Opportunities

Beginner

Students' Book

Michael Harris

David Mower

Longman

CONTENTS

MODULE TOPIC	LANGUAGE	SKILLS
9 EXCURSIONS (p. 61)	**Vocabulary:** places; transport; activities; clothes **Grammar: Present Continuous** **Present Continuous – questions** **Prepositions:** by (car, etc.) at; in; on (place)	**Reading and Listening:** dialogues **Speaking:** transport; phone conversations; clothes
Communication Workshop (p. 66): **Reading and Writing** tourist information **Speaking** a speaking game		
10 WILDLIFE (p. 67)	**Vocabulary:** animals; places; adjectives; parts of animals **Grammar:** *must/mustn't;* subject/object pronouns **Prepositions:** *next to; near*	**Reading and Listening:** dialogues **Speaking:** talking about animals; talking about rules; animal quiz
Communication Workshop (p. 72): **Reading and Writing** a description of an animal **Speaking** talking about an animal **Review** (p. 73): **Grammar and Vocabulary** revision **Pronunciation:** main stress **Culture Corner 5** (p. 74): British Wildlife **Learning Power!** (p. 74): Check your language		
11 MEMORIES (p. 75)	**Vocabulary:** months; ordinal numbers; dates; adjectives; weather; times **Grammar:** *was/were; was/were – questions* **Prepositions:** *on* (dates) on; at; in (time)	**Reading and Listening:** dialogues **Speaking:** saying birthdays; talking about the past; talking about times/first memories
Communication Workshop (p. 80): **Reading and Writing** first day at school **Speaking** memories		
12 AT NIGHT (p. 81)	**Vocabulary:** meals and times; places; TV programmes **Grammar:** *was/were + time expressions; there was/there were* **Prepositions:** *before; after*	**Reading and Listening:** dialogues; TV guide **Speaking:** day and night people; 'alibi' game; TV programmes
Communication Workshop (p. 86): **Reading and Writing** an e-mail message **Speaking** a night out **Review** (p. 87): **Grammar and Vocabulary** revision **Pronunciation:** /ɒ/ and /əʊ/ **Culture Corner 6** (p. 88): Television in Britain **Learning Power!** (p. 88): Do you remember?		
13 ACCIDENTS (p. 89)	**Vocabulary:** emergency services; international words; verbs; road safety **Grammar: Past Simple (regular and irregular verbs)** **Prepositions:** *at; for; off; to; up*	**Reading and Listening:** story order; dialogues; road safety **Speaking:** comparing health services; re-telling a story; talking about past events
Communication Workshop (p. 94): **Reading and Writing** a story **Speaking** telling a story		
14 MISSING HOME (p. 95)	**Vocabulary:** objects; weather; food; adjectives; seasons **Grammar: comparatives** *er/ier (than); more (than)* **Prepositions:** *in; at*	**Reading and Listening:** dialogues; magazine page **Speaking:** comparing opinions; likes and dislikes
Communication Workshop (p. 100): **Reading and Writing** a postcard **Speaking** a discussion **Review** (p. 101): **Grammar and Vocabulary** revision **Pronunciation:** /ð/ and /θ/ **Culture Corner 7** (p. 102): Strange but True **Learning Power!** (p. 102): Using a dictionary		
15 TESTS (p. 103)	**Vocabulary:** qualities; adjectives (feelings) **Grammar:** *going to* for future plans; *have/has to, don't/doesn't have to* **Prepositions:** review of time, place and movement	**Reading and Listening:** exam tips; dialogues; games shows **Speaking:** a questionnaire; diary game; talking about rules
Communication Workshop (p. 108): **Reading and Writing** a quiz **Speaking** a team game		
16 GOODBYE (p. 109)	**Vocabulary:** actions; food and drink; music **Grammar: suggestions** *(Why don't we...?/ Let's ...); revision of verb forms* **Prepositions:** *at; in* (places)	**Reading and Listening:** dialogues **Speaking:** saying goodbye (formal/informal); making suggestions
Communication Workshop (p. 114): **Reading and Writing** party poster **Speaking** roleplay **Review** (p. 115): **Grammar and Vocabulary** revision **Pronunciation:** /d/ and /t/ **Culture Corner 8** (p. 116): Multicultural Britain **Learning Power!** (p. 116): Self-evaluation and Revision		
Extra Time! (pp. 117-125)		
Story Spot: Money Talks by O. Henry (pp. 126-127)		
Communication Workshop roleplay information (p. 128)		

3

Classroom Language

INSTRUCTIONS

🔊 Look and listen.

1 Write.

My name is Amanda.

2 Talk/Say/Tell.

3 Read.

4 Listen.

5 Ask questions.

a book

a book

6 Repeat.

7 Find.

8 Match.

9 Look at.

10 Work in pairs.

11 Complete.

My name is

12 Check.

13 Correct.

Thirtene Thirteen

14 Answer.

One Two Three

Four

THE ALPHABET

🔊 Listen and repeat.

A,a B,b C,c D,d

E,e F,f G,g H,h

I,i J,j K,k L,l

M,m N,n O,o P,p

Q,q R,r S,s T,t

U,u V,v W,w X,x

Y,y Z,z

NUMBERS

🔊 Listen and repeat.

1 one	2 two
3 three	4 four
5 five	6 six
7 seven	8 eight
9 nine	10 ten
11 eleven	12 twelve
13 thirteen	14 fourteen
15 fifteen	16 sixteen
17 seventeen	18 eighteen
19 nineteen	20 twenty

Paola

Gabriela

Kostas

Adam

1 Hello

In this module you ...

- **Talk about** your favourites and meet people.
- **Read** and **listen to** a dialogue.
- **Read** and **write** an e-mail message.
- **Learn about** the verb *to be* (singular).

Warm-up

 pages 2–3

1 Find your country in the Mini-dictionary.

2 Now find the countries in the Key Words box.

KEY WORDS: Countries

Argentina, Britain, Greece, Italy, Poland,
Russia, Turkey, the United States

▭▭ Listen and repeat the names.

3 Look at the photos. Guess the countries of the people.

Example
Paola – Italy

▭▭ Listen and check your answers. Listen again and repeat the names.

4 Match the Key Words with the cities below.

1 London, 2 Istanbul, 3 New York, 4 Warsaw,
5 St Petersburg, 6 Rome, 7 Buenos Aires, 8 Athens

Example
1 Britain

5

1 Hi!

Reading and Listening

1 🔊 Read and listen.
Complete the dialogue.

Italy, Poland, Argentina

Gabriela: Hi! I'm Gabriela.
Adam: Hello, I'm Adam.
   I'm from (1) _____ .
   Are you from (2) _____?
Gabriela: No, I'm not from
   (3) _____ .
   I'm from (4) _____ .

to be (I/you)
Presentation

2 Look at the examples with your teacher.

Affirmative	I You	am ('m) are ('re)	from Poland.
Negative	I You	am not ('m not) are not (aren't)	from Italy.
Questions	Am Are	I you	from Italy?
Short Answers	Yes, I **am**. Yes, you **are**. No, I'**m not**. No, you **aren't**.		

🔊 Listen and repeat.

Practice

3 Write sentences.

Example
1 *I am from Britain.*

1 I/Britain   4 You/Argentina
2 You/Italy   5 I/Poland
3 I/the United States 6 You/Russia

Now write the sentences in the negative.

Example
1 *I am not from Britain.*

4 Write the questions.

Example
1 *Are you from Britain?*

1 No, I'm from Greece.
2 Yes, I'm from Australia.
3 No, I'm from Russia.
4 Yes, I'm from Poland.
5 No, I'm from Italy.
6 Yes, I'm from Argentina.

5 Work in pairs. Student A: choose a country.
Student B: ask questions.

Example
B: Are you from the United States?
A: No, I'm not.
B: Are you from Britain?
A: Yes, I am.

What?/Where? (I/my, you/your)
Presentation

6 🔘 Read and listen. Complete the dialogue.

from, Hi, name, Hello

Kostas: (1) _____ ! I'm Kostas. What's your name?
Paola: (2) _____ . My (3) _____'s Paola.
 Where are you from?
Kostas: I'm from Greece. And you?
Paola: I'm (4) _____ Italy.

7 Look at the examples with your teacher.

Subject Pronouns	Possessive Adjectives
I'm Kostas.	My name's Paola.
Where are you from?	What's your name?

🔘 Listen and repeat the examples.

Practice

8 Work in pairs. Act out the dialogue.

Example
A: Hi! My name's Sue. What's your name?
B: Hello. My name's Tim. I'm from Britain. Where are you from?
A: I'm from the United States. I'm from New York.

Now act out the dialogue again with your names.

Prepositions **from**

9 Look at the examples and write sentences.

Example
Where are you from? Are you from London?
I'm not from Italy. I'm from Argentina.

Example
1 *I'm from Poland.*

1 Adam — from/I'm/ Poland.

2 Paola — you/Where/ from?/are

not/the United States./from/I'm

3 Gabriela

Greece./from/I'm

4 Kostas

5 Gabriela

You/from/aren't/ Argentina.

6 Adam

from/you/Are/Italy?

👉 Now do *Extra Time 1* on page 117.

2 Penfriends

Before you start

pages 2–3

1 Find your nationality.

2 Look at the Key Words. Write the countries.

Example
British – Britain

KEY WORDS: Nationalities

British, American, Argentinian, Greek, Italian, Polish, Russian, Turkish

[°°] Listen and repeat the Key Words.

Reading and Listening

3 [°°] Read and listen to Gabriela.

Complete the table with her favourite stars.

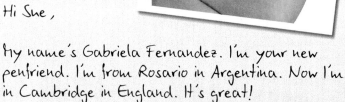

favourite film star
_____
favourite pop star
_____
favourite sports star
_____

Hi Sue,

My name's Gabriela Fernandez. I'm your new penfriend. I'm from Rosario in Argentina. Now I'm in Cambridge in England. It's great!

My favourite film star is from the States. His name's Keanu Reeves and he's great! My favourite pop star is Jennifer Lopez. She's American - she's a film star and a pop star. My favourite sports star isn't American. She's from Slovakia. Her name is Martina Hingis.

Who's your favourite star? Is he or she from the United States?
Write soon.

Gabriela.

to be (he/she/it)
Presentation

4 Look at the examples with your teacher.

Affirmative	He She It	**is ('s)**	great!
Negative	He She It	**is not (isn't)**	American.
Questions	**Is**	he/she/it	from the States?
Short Answers	Yes, he/she/it **is.** No, he/she/it **isn't.**		

[°°] Listen and repeat the examples.

Practice

5 Use the words to write sentences.

Example
Brad Pitt isn't Russian. He's American.

1   Brad Pitt/Russia/the United States
2   Kate Winslet/Canada/Britain
3   Martina Hingis/Poland/Slovakia
4   Jennifer Lopez/Argentina/the United States
5   Arnold Schwarzenegger/Germany/Austria
6   Michael Schumacher/France/Germany

6   Write five questions about the nationalities of stars.

Example
Is Venus Williams Canadian?

Now work in pairs. Ask and answer your questions.

Example
A: *Is Venus Williams Canadian?*
B: *No, she isn't. She's from the States.*

7   Work in pairs. Student A: choose a star.
Student B: ask questions. Guess the person.

A: *Is it a film star?*
B: *Yes, it is.*
A: *Is it a woman?*
B: *No, it isn't.*
A: *OK, he's a man. Is he American?*
B: *Yes, he is.*
A: *Is it Brad Pitt?*
B: *Yes, it is!!!*

Reading and Listening

8   Read and listen. Complete the dialogue.

pop star, music, film star

Paola: Who's your favourite (1) _____?
Gabriela: His name is Keanu Reeves. He's great!
Paola: Where's he from?
Gabriela: He's from the States.
Paola: And who's your favourite (2) _____?
Gabriela: Her name is Jennifer Lopez. She's a
      (3) _____ and a (4) _____ .
Paola: What's your favourite (5) _____?
Gabriela: My favourite (6) _____ is 'soul'.

Who?/What?/Where? (*he/his, she/her, it/its*)

Presentation

9 Look at the examples with your teacher.

Questions

Who's your favourite star?
Where's he from?
What's your favourite music?

Subject Pronouns	Possessive Adjectives
He's great.	**His** name is Keanu Reeves.
She's from Slovakia.	**Her** name is Martina Hingis.
It's great.	**Its** name is Cambridge.

Listen and repeat the examples.

Practice

10 Write sentences about your favourite:

pop star, film star, sports star, music

Example
My favourite pop star is from Puerto Rico.
His name is Ricky Martin.

11 Work in pairs. Ask and answer questions about your favourite stars.

Example
A: *Who's your favourite sports star?*
B: *My favourite star is Rivaldo. He's from Brazil.*

☞ Now do *Extra Time 2* on page 117.

Communication Workshop

Writing: An e-mail

1 Correct the e-mail. Write the capital letters.

Example
Tom

Hi tom,
My name's adam nowak. I'm your new penfriend. I'm from toruń – it's in poland.
My favourite film star is from the united states. Her name's cameron diaz and she's great! My favourite pop star is Beck. He's american. My favourite sports star isn't american. He's from brazil. His name is rivaldo. My favourite music is 'heavy metal'. What's your favourite music? Who's your favourite pop star? Where is he or she from?
Write soon.

adam

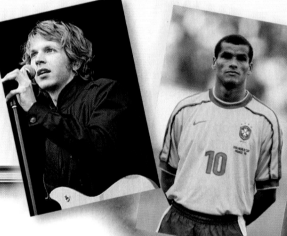

Write an e-mail. Follow the stages.

Stage 1
Complete the table about you.

1 name
2 nationality/from
3 favourite film star
4 favourite sports star
5 favourite music
6 favourite pop star

Stage 2
Now write your e-mail to a penfriend.

Speaking: A Roleplay

Talk about personal information. Follow the stages.

Stage 1
Look at the table in Stage 1 of the Writing Workshop. Write questions.

Example
1 *What's your name?*

Stage 2
Work in pairs. Ask and answer the questions.

Example
A: *Hi! What's your name?*
B: *My name's _____ .*

Talkback
Tell the class about your partner.

Example
Her favourite sports star is David Beckham.

2 Meet the family

In this module you ...

- Talk about families.
- Read and listen to a dialogue.
- Read and write about a family.
- Learn about the verb *to be* (plural), possessive *'s*, and *a/an*.

Warm-up

page 1

1 Check the meaning of the Key Words.

KEY WORDS: Families

daughter, father, grandfather, grandmother, mother, son

[○○] Listen and repeat.

2 Look at the photo. Match the people and the Key Words.

Example 1 *daughter*

Match the people with the ages.

a) 15, b) 40, c) 45, d) 65, e) 73, f) 17

Example *daughter a)*

3 [○○] Listen and repeat the numbers.

21 23 29 30 38 40 44 49 50 57
60 62 70 77 80 86 90 95 100 101

4 Bingo. Choose six numbers (1–50). Write them in the table.

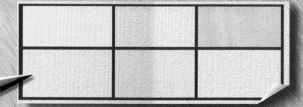

[○○] Listen to the numbers. The first person with all the numbers is the winner!

3 Our Family

Before you start

page 1

1 Check the meaning of the Key Words.

KEY WORDS: Families
wife/husband, parents/children(kids), brother/sister

Listen and repeat.

Reading and Listening

2 Read and listen. Match the people with the Key Words.

1 Jamie/Megan, 2 Mr/Mrs Williams,
3 Jamie and Megan/Mr and Mrs Williams

Mrs Williams: Hello. Come in. I'm Mrs Williams.
Gabriela: Hello, my name's Gabriela.
Paola: And I'm Paola.
Mrs Williams: Where are you from?
Paola: I'm from Italy and Gabriela is from Argentina.
Mrs Williams: Great! We're from Wales.
Paola: Really?
Mrs Williams: Yes. We aren't from Cambridge. But welcome to Cambridge!
Paola and Gabriela: Thanks.
Mrs Williams: Our children aren't here now.
Gabriela: Are they at school?
Mrs Williams: No, they aren't. They're at the cinema.

to be (PLURAL)
Presentation

3 Look at the examples with your teacher.

Affirmative	We You They	are ('re)	from Wales.
Negative	We You They	are not (aren't)	from Cambridge.
Questions	Are	we/you/they	at school?
Short Answers	Yes, we/you/they **are**. No, we/you/they **aren't**.		

Listen and repeat.

Practice

4 Write sentences.

Example
1 *They are not from Britain.*

1 Gabriela and Paola/from Britain
2 Gabriela and Paola/sisters
3 Mr and Mrs Williams/from Wales
4 Mr and Mrs Williams/from Cambridge
5 Jamie and Megan/at home
6 Jamie and Megan/at the cinema

5 Work in groups of four. In pairs, choose a place. Ask and answer questions.

Example
A/B: *Are you from Britain?*
C/D: *No, we aren't.*
A/B: *Are you American?*
C/D: *Yes, we are.*
A/B: *Are you from New York?*
C/D: *Yes, we are!*

Reading and Listening

6 Read and listen. Complete the dialogue.

grandparents, sisters (x2), parents

Paola: Where are you from in Wales?
Mrs Williams: We're from Cardiff. Where are you from in Italy?
Paola: Well, my (1) _____ and I are from Siena. We are from Tuscany. Our (2) _____ are from Rome.
Mrs Williams: What are their names?
Paola: Pia and Mauricio. And my (3) _____ are Cristina and Susana.
Mrs Williams: How old are they?
Paola: Cristina's twelve and Susana's ten. They aren't at school now. They are with our (4) _____ in Rome.

How old? (we/our, you/your, they/their)
Presentation

7 Look at the examples with your teacher.

Subject Pronouns	Possessive Adjectives
We are from Tuscany.	**Our** parents are from Rome.
Where are **you** from?	What are **your** names?
They are not at school now.	What are **their** names?

Question: How old ...

How old are they? Cristina's twelve and Susana's ten.

Listen and repeat.

Practice

8 Complete the dialogue with these words:

I, your, we, their, her, you, our

A: What are (1) _____ names?
B: I'm Megan.
C: And (2) _____ 'm Jamie. I'm (3) _____ brother.
A: Where are (4) _____ from?
C: (5) _____ 're from Cambridge. (6) _____ parents are from Wales.
A: What are (7) _____ names?
B: Alice and David.
A: How old are you?
B: I'm fifteen and Jamie's seventeen.

9 Write sentences about your family:

where from – names – how old

Example
We are from São Paulo. My grandfather is from Bahia. His name is Luis. He's 73. My father is 42. His name is Roberto. My mother ...

Work in pairs. Ask and answer questions about your families.

☞ Now do *Extra Time 3* on page 118.

4 My Family

pages 4–5

Before you start

1 🔊 What Key Words are similar in your language? Listen and repeat the Key Words.

KEY WORDS: Jobs

actor/actress, engineer, businessman/woman, doctor, student, teacher

2 Look at the photos. What Key Words can you see?

Reading and Listening

3 🔊 Read and listen. Write their names.

(mother)

(father)

(son)

Adam

(son)

My Family   Adam Nowak

Our surname is Nowak. We are from Toruń in Poland. My dad and my grandmother are from Kraków. My grandfather is from Warsaw. He is a doctor.

My father's name is Tomasz. He is an engineer and he is forty-nine. Dad's favourite film star is Meryl Streep.

My mum is a businesswoman. Her name is Anna and she is forty-three years old. Her favourite pop stars are The Bee Gees. Mum's favourite music is not heavy metal!!!

My brother's name is Mirek. He is a student at university in Warsaw. He is twenty years old. Mirek's favourite star is Sandra Bullock. She is an actress.

I am seventeen. I am at school. My favourite pop group is AC/DC. AC/DC's music is great!

4 What are the jobs of these people?

Anna, Sandra Bullock, Meryl Streep, Adam's grandfather, Tomasz, Adam

Example
Anna is a businesswoman.

---

a/an
Presentation

5 Look at the examples with your teacher.

a	He is **a** doctor.
	My mum is **a** businesswoman.
an	He is **an** engineer.
	She is **an** actress.

Listen and repeat.

Practice

 pages 4–5

6 Check the meaning of the Key Words. Match *a* or *an* with the Key Words.

Example
an architect

KEY WORDS: Jobs

architect, computer programmer, electrician, model, housewife, scientist, secretary

7 Read the sentences about Jamie's family. Put in *a/an* where necessary.

Example
a sports teacher

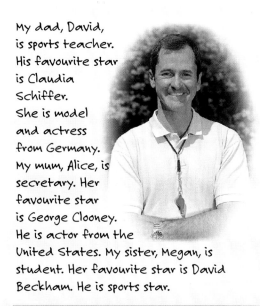

My dad, David, is sports teacher. His favourite star is Claudia Schiffer. She is model and actress from Germany. My mum, Alice, is secretary. Her favourite star is George Clooney. He is actor from the United States. My sister, Megan, is student. Her favourite star is David Beckham. He is sports star.

POSSESSIVE: 's
Presentation

8 Look at the examples with your teacher.

Dad**'s** favourite film star is Meryl Streep.
Mum**'s** favourite music is not heavy metal.
Mirek**'s** favourite star is Sandra Bullock.
Adam**'s** grandfather is a doctor.

Listen and repeat.

Practice

9 Write sentences. Are the sentences true (T) or false (F)?
Example
1 *Adam's family is from Poland. T*

1 Adam/family/from Poland
2 His family/surname/Nowak
3 His dad/name/Sam
4 His mum/favourite pop stars/The Bee Gees
5 His brother/name/Mirek
6 Adam/favourite pop stars/Backstreet Boys

10 Write sentences about the people in your family.

names – jobs – favourite star

Example
My mum's name is Susan. She is a teacher. Her favourite star is Bruce Springsteen.

Work in pairs. Ask and answer the questions.

What is your mum's name?
What is your mum's job?
Who is her favourite star?

Prepositions **at**

11 Look at the example of *at*.

Example
*He is a student **at** university.*

Complete the sentences with *at* or *from*.

1 My brother is _____ university in London.
2 My family is _____ Britain.
3 I am _____ school now.
4 My teacher is _____ Bristol.
5 My mum is _____ home now.
6 She is _____ Liverpool.

☛ Now do *Extra Time 4* on page 118.

Module 2

Communication Workshop

Writing: A Family

1 Read about Kostas's family. Put in capital letters and full stops.

Example
Our surname is Dimitriou. We are ...

My Family by Kostas Dimitriou
our surname is Dimitriou we are from Rhodes in
Greece my mother's name is Katerina she is a
translator she is thirty-eight mum's favourite
film star is Pierce Brosnan my dad
is a doctor his name is Nikos and he is forty
years old his favourite pop stars are The Rolling
Stones dad's favourite music is not Frank Sinatra!
my sisters are Maria and Eleni Maria is thirteen and Eleni is ten
Maria's favourite pop star is Bon Jovi Eleni's favourite is Ricky Martin
I am sixteen I am a student my favourite pop star is Britney Spears
Britney's music is great!

Write about your family or invent a family. Follow the stages.

Stage 1
Copy and complete the table about your family.

Name	from	age	occupation	favourite stars

Stage 2
Use your table to write about your family. Use Kostas's profile to help you.

Stage 3
Check your writing for these things:

verb *to be* ✓ pronouns ✓
punctuation (capital letters and full stops) ✓

Write your description neatly and add a photo.

Speaking: Families

Ask and answer questions about families. Follow the stages.

Stage 1
Write the people in your family, e.g. mother, father, brother. Give the list to your partner.

Stage 2
Work in pairs. Ask and answer questions.

Example
What's your sister's name?

Talkback
Tell the class interesting things about your partner.

Example
Jane's grandfather is an actor.

Review

Grammar

1 Complete the description with these words:

I, my (x5), he, his, she, her, their

(1) _____ name is Kelly. (2) _____ am from Miami in the United States. (3) _____ family's surname is O'Connell. (4) _____ grandparents are from Ireland. (5) _____ names are Patrick and Carol. (6) _____ mum's name is Fiona. (7) _____ is a doctor and (8) _____ favourite group is The Corrs. (9) _____ brother's name is Michael. (10) _____ is at university and (11) _____ favourite group is Pearl Jam.

2 Use the diagram to write sentences about Jamie's family.

Example
His family's surname is Williams. His parents are from Wales. His mum's ...

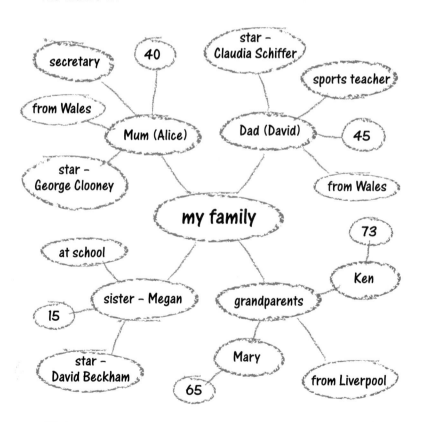

3 Write questions for the answers.

1 Yes, I'm British.
2 From Birmingham.
3 Johnson.
4 Eighteen.
5 No, I'm at university.
6 My dad's name is Chris.
7 He's a teacher.
8 My favourite star's Tom Cruise.
9 She's from Argentina.

Vocabulary

4 Write the nationalities for these countries:

Germany, Poland, the United States, Spain, Argentina, Russia

5 Write the numbers.

Example
1 *eighty-five*

1 68 + 17 = _____
2 76 – 53 = _____
3 14 x 4 = _____
4 19 + 68 = _____
5 55 – 28 = _____
6 9 x 11 = _____

6 Identify the jobs and the family words.

1 htrerbo b_____
2 oorcdt d_____
3 nemssansiub b_____
4 tssier s_____
5 cresartye s_____

Pronunciation: Word Stress

7 🔊 Listen to the words. Mark the number of syllables.

Example
Argentina Ar gen ti na (4)

Argentina, music, penfriend, Poland, father, school, seventeen, grandmother, student, son, fifteen, family, Brazil, favourite, American, great, daughter, twenty, Turkey, nine, teacher, university, engineer, film, Italy

8 🔊 Listen again. Identify the main stress.

Example
Argen**ti**na

Listen to the words and repeat them.

Names in Britain

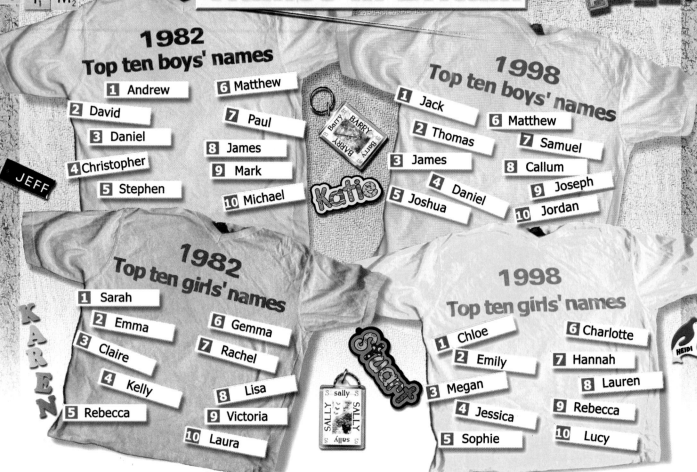

J₈ I₁ M₂

PETER

1982 Top ten boys' names

1. Andrew
2. David
3. Daniel
4. Christopher
5. Stephen
6. Matthew
7. Paul
8. James
9. Mark
10. Michael

JEFF

BARRY

Katie

1998 Top ten boys' names

1. Jack
2. Thomas
3. James
4. Daniel
5. Joshua
6. Matthew
7. Samuel
8. Callum
9. Joseph
10. Jordan

1982 Top ten girls' names

1. Sarah
2. Emma
3. Claire
4. Kelly
5. Rebecca
6. Gemma
7. Rachel
8. Lisa
9. Victoria
10. Laura

KAREN

Stuart

sally SALLY

1998 Top ten girls' names

1. Chloe
2. Emily
3. Megan
4. Jessica
5. Sophie
6. Charlotte
7. Hannah
8. Lauren
9. Rebecca
10. Lucy

HEIDI

1 🔈 Look at the lists. Listen and repeat the names.

2 Match these names with the names on the lists:

Andy, Dave, Chris, Steve, Mike, Becky, Vicky, Meg, Tom, Jess

3 What are five popular girls' and boys' names in your country?

List five very common surnames.

Learning Power!

Classroom Language

1 Look at the questions. Ask and answer questions about words from this module.

What's *film star* in Spanish?
(or Polish/Russian/Greek etc.)
What's _____ in English?

2 🔈 Listen and repeat.

Sorry? Can you repeat that, please?

3 Work in pairs. Say sentences. Ask your partner to repeat.

Example
A: *My family is from Cambridge.*
B: *Sorry. Can you repeat that, please?*
A: *Yes. My family is from Cambridge.*

3 At home

In this module you ...

- **Talk about** houses and rooms.
- **Read** and **listen to** dialogues and a letter.
- **Write** a description of your house and room.
- **Learn about** *have got*, *has got* and *the*.

Warm-up

pages 6–7

1 🔊 Check the meaning of the Key Words. Listen and repeat.

KEY WORDS: HOMES

bath, bed, carpet, cooker, fridge, lamp, shower, sofa, table, television (TV), toilet, video, window

What Key Words can you see in the photos?

2 Put the Key Words in the correct column.

Sitting room	Bedroom	Kitchen	Bathroom
sofa			

3 🔊 Spelling Test. Close your books. Listen and write down the words.

Prepositions **in**

4 Work in groups. Take turns to think of an object in a house. The others guess the object.

Example
A: *Is it **in** the sitting room?*
B: *No.*
C: *Is it **in** the kitchen?*
B: *Yes.*
D: *Is it a fridge?*
B: *Yes!*

Module 3

5 Our House

Before you start

A–Z

1 [cassette icon] Check the meaning of the Key Words. Listen and repeat.

> ### KEY WORDS: Adjectives
> bad, big, boring, good, interesting, new, old, small

2 Put the Key Words in pairs of opposites.

Example
bad – good

Look at these sentences.

It's a **new** computer.
It's an **old** computer.

Reading and Listening

A–Z

3 Read the dialogue. Check the meaning of new words.

Megan: Well, we've got a sitting room with a (1) _____ TV. You've got a TV in your bedroom, too. It's an (2) _____ TV but it's OK.

Gabriela: Have we got a video?

Megan: No, you haven't. The video is in the sitting room. This is Mum and Dad's (3) _____ computer. They haven't got (4) _____ games, but they've got an (5) _____ CD for you to learn English.

Paola: Thanks. Have you got a garden?

Megan: Yes, we've got a (6) _____ garden.

Paola: Great. We haven't got a garden at home.

Megan: And I've got a dog, Toby. He's in the garden now.

Paola: I haven't got a dog. I've got a cat. Have you got a pet, Gabriela?

Gabriela: Yes, I have. I've got two dogs called Mili and Pili!

4 [cassette icon] Read and listen. Complete the gaps with Key Words.

20

have got (*I, you, we, they*)
Presentation

5 Look at the examples with your teacher.

Affirmative		
I/You/We/They **have ('ve) got**		a dog.
Negative		
I/You/We/They **have not (haven't) got**		a garden.
Questions		
Have	I/you/we/they **got**	a video?
Short Answers		
Yes, I/you/we/they	**have.**	
No, I/you/we/they	**haven't.**	

🔊 Listen and repeat.

Practice

6 Complete the sentences with *have* or *haven't*.

A: I (1) __*have*__ got a new computer. (2) _____ you got a computer in your bedroom?
B: No, I (3) _____ got a computer in my bedroom. My parents (4) _____ got a computer in the sitting room. (5) _____ you got a pet?
A: Yes, I (6) _____ . I (7) _____ got a dog.

7 Write five sentences about your home.

cat, computer, dog, garden, video

Example
We've got a small dog. We haven't got a computer.

8 Write questions.

Example
Have you got a pet?

1 you/a pet?
2 your parents/a television?
3 you/big bedroom?
4 your parents/a car?
5 you/a CD player?

Now work in pairs. Ask and answer the questions.

Example
A: *Have you got a pet?*
B: *Yes, I have. I've got a dog.*

the AND *a/an*
Presentation

9 Look at the examples with your teacher.

Articles	
a/an	**the**
It's **an** old TV.	**The** TV is in the bedroom.
Have we got **a** video?	**The** video is in the sitting room.
We've got **a** small garden.	The dog is in **the** garden now.

🔊 Listen and repeat.

10 🔊 Listen to two ways you can pronounce *the*.

1 the garden
2 the exam

🔊 Listen and repeat.

1 the teacher, the computer, the bedroom
2 the English teacher, the information, the art lesson

Practice

11 Complete the sentences with *a*, *an* or *the*.

We live in (1) _____ old house. We've got (2) _____ cat and (3) _____ dog. (4) _____ cat is called Tibbs and (5) _____ dog is called Lara. We've got (6) _____ big garden. Tibbs is in (7) _____ garden now. Lara is in (8) _____ house.

☞ Now do *Extra Time 5* on page 118.

6 My Room

Before you start

1 🔊 Listen and repeat. Match the Key Words with the colours.

KEY WORDS: Colours

black, blue, green, orange, pink, red, white, yellow

Reading and Listening

2 🔊 Read and listen to Gabriela's letter to an American friend. Are the sentences true (T) or false (F)?

1 Her friend's name is Kelly.
2 Gabriela and Paola have got a computer in their bedroom.
3 The bedroom window is small.
4 Her friend's brother's name is Andy.

Dear Kelly,

How are you? Are the dogs OK?

I'm with the Williams family - Megan and her brother Jamie, and their parents. They've got a dog. The house is nice. It's got a big sitting room, a kitchen, a bathroom and four bedrooms. I'm in a bedroom with Paola, an Italian student. She's great. She hasn't got a dog in Italy - she's got a cat called Leo. Mrs Williams has got a computer in the sitting room and Jamie has got great CDs.

Our bedroom has got white walls. It's got posters of dogs on the wall. It hasn't got a big window. It's got shelves for our books, papers and CDs. It's got a new, black desk with a yellow lamp - it's great.

Write soon!
Love,
Gabriela.
PS: Has your brother Tom got his new computer?

has got (he, she, it)
Presentation

3 Look at the examples with your teacher.

Affirmative

He/She/It	**has ('s) got**	great CD games.

Negative

He/She	**has not (hasn't) got**	a dog.
It	**has not (hasn't) got**	a big window.

Questions

Has	he/she/it	**got** a good report?

Short Answers

Yes, he/she/it	**has.**
No, he/she/it	**hasn't.**

🔊 Listen and repeat.

Practice

4 Complete the sentences with *have/has* (+), *haven't/hasn't* (–) or *have/has* (?).

1 I _____ got a small room. (+)
2 We _____ got a big house. (–)
3 My room _____ got a big window. (–)
4 _____ you got a video?
5 My sister _____ got a piano. (+)
6 _____ your brother got a computer?
7 They _____ got a cat. (–)
8 We _____ got a big garden. (+)

5 Write sentences about your room.

white walls, posters of dogs, a big window, shelves, a desk, a lamp, a computer

Example
It hasn't got white walls.
It has got posters of dogs.

Now work in pairs. Ask your partner about his/her room.

Example
A: *Has it got white walls?*
B: *No, it hasn't. It has got blue walls.*

6 Work in groups. Play the game.

Example
Adam: I've got a computer.
Paola: Adam's got a computer and I've got a cat.
Kostas: Adam's got a computer, Paola's got a cat and I've got a camera.
Gabriela: Adam's got a computer, Paola's got a cat, Kostas's got a camera and I've got two dogs.

Listening

7 ⦿ Listen and complete the dialogue with the phone number.

Gabriela: Hello?
Kostas: Hi, Gabriela. It's me, Kostas.
Gabriela: Hi! Is your English friend's house nice?
Kostas: Yes. It's great.
Gabriela: What's your home phone number?
Kostas: My number is _____ . Give me a call.
Gabriela: OK, bye!

Speaking

8 **Roleplay**. Work in pairs. Phone your partner and ask for his/her home phone number.

☞ Now do *Extra Time 6* on page 118.

Communication Workshop

Writing: Description of a Room

1 Find this sentence in Gabriela's letter in Lesson 6. Put in the commas.

It's got a big sitting room a kitchen a bathroom and four bedrooms.

2 Read Kostas's description of his room in Greece. Put in the commas.

> My room has got white walls. It's got shelves for my books CDs and cassettes. I've got posters of my favourite stars on the wall – Britney Spears Arnold Schwarzenegger and Ryan Giggs. I've got a desk for my computer.

Write a description of your room. Follow the stages.

Stage 1
Write notes about your room.

Example
walls – blue – posters, photos
carpet – red
shelves – books, cassette player

Stage 2
Write a description.

Stage 3
Check your writing for punctuation:

capital letters and full stops ✓
apostrophes in contractions ✓
commas in lists ✓

Speaking: Quiz

Test your friends. Follow the stages.

Stage 1
In groups, read the descriptions of your rooms.

Stage 2
Individually, write true/false sentences about the rooms.

Example
John's house has got five bedrooms.

Stage 3
Work in groups. Take turns to say sentences about the rooms. The other students say 'true' or 'false'.

Example
A: *Petros has got a computer in his bedroom.*
B: *False.*
A: *No, it's true!*

4 At school

In this module you ...

- **Talk about** your classroom and lessons.
- **Read** and **listen to** dialogues.
- **Read** and **write about** an ideal school.
- **Learn about** singular and plural nouns and *this, that, these* and *those*.

Warm-up

 page 8

1 🔊 Listen and repeat.

KEY WORDS: The Classroom

desk, board, shelf, box, clock, poster, wall, floor, bag, pen, cupboard, chair

2 Match the Key Words with the things in the photo.

3 Put the letters of the alphabet in the correct order.

f	b	a	e	c	k	d	g	j
h	l	i	m	o	q	n	p	u
s	r	z	w	t	v	x	y

🔊 Now listen and check your answer. Repeat the letters.

4 Write the Key Words in alphabetical order.

5 🔊 Spelling Game. Listen to the teacher on the cassette. Put your hand up when you know the word.

Example
Teacher: *T-w-e ...*
Student 1: *Twenty?*
Teacher: *No. T-w-e-l ...*
Student 2: *Twelve?*
Teacher: *Yes!*

7 Lessons

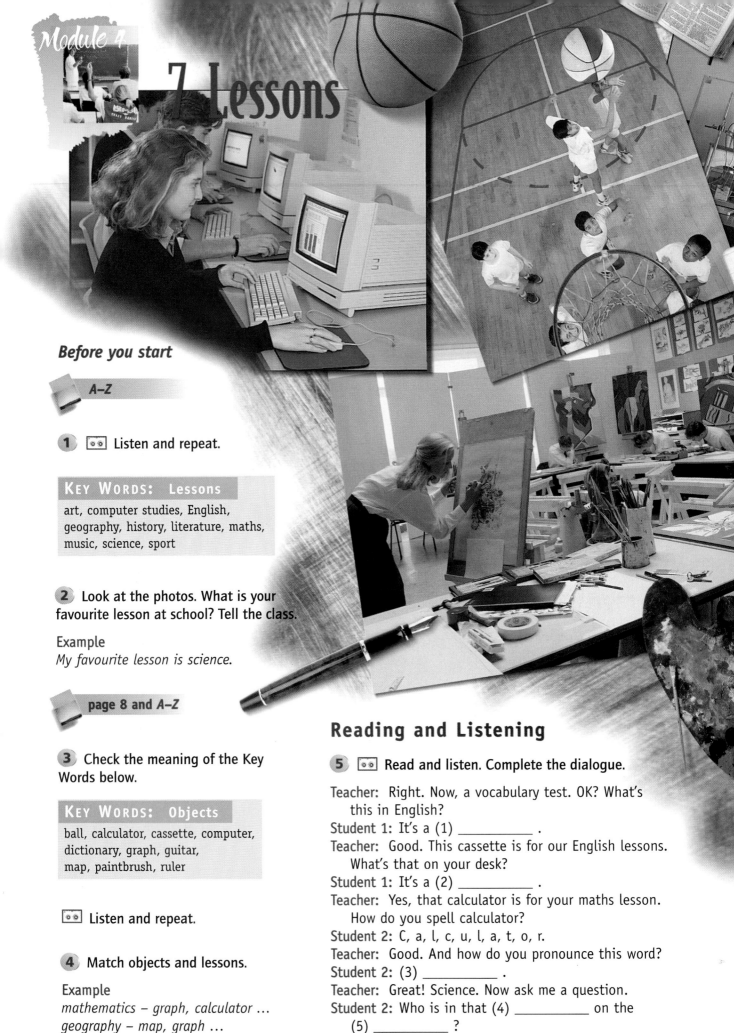

Before you start

A–Z

1 Listen and repeat.

KEY WORDS: Lessons

art, computer studies, English, geography, history, literature, maths, music, science, sport

2 Look at the photos. What is your favourite lesson at school? Tell the class.

Example
My favourite lesson is science.

page 8 and A–Z

3 Check the meaning of the Key Words below.

KEY WORDS: Objects

ball, calculator, cassette, computer, dictionary, graph, guitar, map, paintbrush, ruler

Listen and repeat.

4 Match objects and lessons.

Example
mathematics – graph, calculator ...
geography – map, graph ...

Reading and Listening

5 Read and listen. Complete the dialogue.

Teacher: Right. Now, a vocabulary test. OK? What's this in English?
Student 1: It's a (1) _____ .
Teacher: Good. This cassette is for our English lessons. What's that on your desk?
Student 1: It's a (2) _____ .
Teacher: Yes, that calculator is for your maths lesson. How do you spell calculator?
Student 2: C, a, l, c, u, l, a, t, o, r.
Teacher: Good. And how do you pronounce this word?
Student 2: (3) _____ .
Teacher: Great! Science. Now ask me a question.
Student 2: Who is in that (4) _____ on the (5) _____ ?
Teacher: That's Pierce Brosnan. He's an Irish film star.

this/that
Presentation

6 Look at the examples with your teacher.

Singular
this cassette 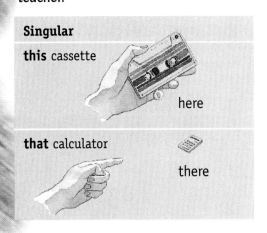
here
that calculator
there

🔊 Listen and repeat.

Practice

7 Write *this* or *that* with the pictures.

1 _____ clock.

2 _____ dictionary.

3 _____ ruler.

4 _____ computer.

8 Complete the sentences with *this* or *that*.

1 Pass me _____ dictionary, please.
2 Come here. Look at _____ picture in my book.
3 What is _____ photo here?
4 Give me _____ book, please.

9 Work in pairs. Look at the pictures. Test your partner.

Example
What's this in English? How do you spell it?

10 Work in pairs. Test your partner about things in the classroom.

Example
A: *What's this?*
B: *It's a bag. Who is in that poster?*
A: *It's Shakespeare.*

 *Prepositions* **on**

11 Work in groups. Take turns to say where an object is. The others guess the object. Use these words:

on my desk, **on** the shelf, **on** the wall,
on the floor, **on** the cupboard, **on** the board

Example
A: *It's on the wall.*
B: *The clock?*
A: *No.*
C: *That poster?*
A: *Yes!*

👉 Now do *Extra Time 7* on page 119.

8 Projects

Before you start

A–Z

1 [°°] Listen and repeat.

KEY WORDS: Objects
camera, encyclopedia, magazine,
map, newspaper, pencil, photo,
piece of paper, rubber, watch

Find the objects in the photos.

Reading and Listening

2 [°°] Read and listen. Match the
sentences with the students.

Example
1 *Kostas*

1 Look at these photos. They're great.
2 Adam? Pass those pencils, please.
3 What? These pencils?
4 These magazines are really good!
5 Where are those maps of Cambridge?

these/those
Presentation

3 Look at the examples with
your teacher.

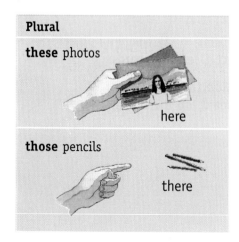

Plural

these photos

here

those pencils

there

[°°] Listen and repeat.

4 Look at the examples with your teacher.

Singular	Plural	Rule
1 bag, desk, pen	bags, desks, pens	add **s**
2 box, watch, paintbrush	boxes, watches, paintbrushes	add **es**
3 dictionary	dictionaries	change **y** to **ies**
4 shelf	shelves	change **f** to **ves**

[°°] Listen and repeat.

Look at the examples with your teacher.

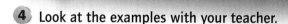

This photo is **great**.	It is a **great** photo.
These magazines are **good**.	They are **good** magazines.

Adjectives are singular.

7 Complete the dialogues with *these* or *those*.

Pass me (1) _____ dictionaries, please.

(2) _____ dictionaries?

Yes, (3) _____ .

(4) _____ maps are good.

(5) _____ maps on the wall?

No, (6) _____ on the desk.

Practice

5 Write the plurals.

Example
these books

1 this book
2 that watch
3 this dictionary
4 this shelf
5 that clock
6 this map
7 that box
8 this chair

6 Write plural sentences.

Example
blue pen – These pens are blue. These are blue pens.

blue pen, good dictionary, red pencil, new watch, old map, interesting magazine

8 Work in pairs. Look at the dialogues in Exercise 7. Act the dialogues. Use these words:

pens, magazines, books, pencils

9 Work in groups. Choose an object in your classroom. Take turns to say the first letter. The others guess the object.

Example
A: *b*
B: *Box?*
A: *No.*
C: *Board?*
A: *Yes!*

☞ Now do *Extra Time 8* on page 119.

Communication Workshop

Writing: My Ideal School

1 Read Paola's ideal school timetable. Correct the spelling mistakes (underlined).

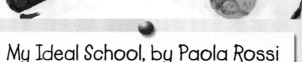

My Ideal School, by Paola Rossi

Day	9.00–10.30	11.00–12.30	13.30–14.30	14.30–16.00
Monday	Matematics	English	History	Sport
Tuesday	Computer studies	Literature	Musik	Art
Wednesday	English	History	Geography	Sport
Thursday	Matematics	Literature	Cience	Cience
Friday	Musik	Musik	Sport	Sport

2 Read the timetable again. What are Paola's favourite lessons?

Write a timetable for your ideal school. Follow the stages.

Stage 1
Draw a timetable. Think about:

- the number of lessons per day
- the times of the lessons

Stage 2
Write your timetable.

Stage 3
Check your work for:

spelling ✓ capital letters ✓

Talkback
In groups, read your timetables. Vote for *one* ideal school.

Speaking: A Vocabulary Quiz

Give your partner a vocabulary quiz. Follow the stages.

Stage 1
Think of ten words and write quiz questions like these:

- *The first letter is …*
- *How do you spell …?*
- *It is on the …*
- *What is … in English?*

Stage 2
Work in pairs. Test your partner's vocabulary. He/She can guess three times.

Example
A: *The first letter is 'c'.*
B: *Cupboard?*
A: *No.*
B: *Chair?*
A: *Yes, one point.*

Review

Grammar

1 Write sentences with *have got* or *has got*: affirmative (+), negative (−) or questions (?).

1 he/a computer (−)
2 Paola/a cat (+)
3 she/a nice bedroom (?)
4 we/a small kitchen (+)
5 you/a ruler (?)
6 they/a car (−)

2 Complete the sentences with *a, an* or *the*.

We've got (1) _____ old house with (2) _____ garden. (3) _____ garden is big.

I've got (4) _____ cat and (5) _____ dog. (6) _____ cat is called Suzy and (7) _____ dog is called Chico.

She's got (8) _____ interesting book for our project. (9) _____ book has got old photos of Cambridge.

3 Complete the sentences with *this, that, these* or *those*.

1 Who are _____ people in the street?
2 What are _____ on my desk?
3 Come here. Look at _____ exercise.
4 Pass me _____ dictionary, please.

4 Write the plural.

1 dictionary   6 watch
2 pen   7 family
3 box   8 paintbrush
4 shelf   9 secretary
5 cassette   10 desk

Vocabulary

5 Write words in the table. You have got three minutes.

Bathroom	Bedroom	Kitchen	Sitting Room
shower	bed	fridge	sofa

Compare your table with a partner's.

6 Find eight colours in the word square.

W	O	L	L	E	Y	R
O	R	E	D	B	E	B
E	A	L	E	R	B	L
T	N	B	U	P	G	A
I	G	R	E	E	N	C
H	E	U	P	I	N	K
W	R	P	E	U	L	B

Now write the colours in alphabetical order.

7 Write your school timetable in English.

Pronunciation

8 🔊 Listen and repeat.

Group 1 /iː/: eat
Group 2 /ɪ/: it

Put these words in the correct group.

fridge, green, teacher, this, these, bin, pink, read, kitchen

🔊 Now listen and check your answers.

9 🔊 Listen and repeat.

brother, father, mother, the, this, that, these, those, they, their

HOMES IN BRITAIN

Each floor of a building is called a storey. A house with one storey is called a **bungalow**.

A **semi-detached house** is connected to one other house.

A **flat** is a set of rooms (including a kitchen and bathroom) inside a large building. This building is called a **block of flats**.

Terraced houses are houses in a line.

A **detached house** is not connected to other houses.

A **cottage** is a small, old house in the country.

1 Read about British homes.

1   What type of house have you got?
2   Has your country got houses like these?

Learning Power!

Vocabulary

1 Look at the picture section of the Mini-dictionary. Find the pages that these words are on.

bag, banana, football, bedroom, lamp, fridge, ruler, poster, wardrobe, pencil, bathroom, teacher, lawyer, sandwich, electrician, tennis, armchair, basketball, waiter

Example
bag – page 8 (at school)

2 Make a vocabulary book.

• You can write words alphabetically, e.g. bag, board, box.
• You can write words by topics, e.g. family, school, houses, sport.
• You can write words by module, e.g. Module 1 'Hello'.

Write this information:

desk   – xxxxxx   His book is on the desk.

word   translation   example sentence

5 Going out

In this module you ...

- Talk about places.
- Read and listen to dialogues.
- Write a description of a place.
- Learn about Imperatives and *some/any*.

Warm-up

 pages 10–11

1 🔘 Check the meaning of the Key Words. Listen and repeat.

KEY WORDS: Places

church, hotel, main square, museum, mosque, park, railway station, restaurant, shop, street

2 Look at the photos of Cambridge. What places can you see?

Example *park*

Prepositions   near

3 Look at the sentences about the map. Are they true (T) or false (F)?

1 The hotel is **near** the main square. (F)
2 The hotel is **near** the railway station.
3 The shops are **near** the park.
4 The restaurant is **near** the hotel.
5 The restaurant is **near** the museum.

4 Work in pairs. Imagine you are in the main square. Say true or false sentences with 'near'.

Example
A: *The museum is near here.*
B: *True!*

9 Where To Go

Before you start

pages 10–11

1 🔊 Check the meaning of the
Key Words. Listen and repeat.

KEY WORDS: Places

bookshop, café, cinema, disco,
market, newsagent's

2 Match the Key Words
with the pictures.

Example
T-shirt – market

3 🔊 Check the meaning of the adjectives.
Listen and repeat.

KEY WORDS: Adjectives

bad, boring, cheap, expensive, fantastic,
good, interesting, terrible

4 Write sentences about places in your area.

bookshop – cheap/expensive
café – fantastic/terrible
cinema – interesting/boring
disco – good/bad

Example
The International Bookshop has got cheap books.
The Castle Bookshop has got expensive books!

Reading and Listening

5 🔲 Read and listen. Complete the dialogues with these adjectives:

cheap, expensive, good, boring, fantastic, interesting

Paola: Has this area got a (1) _____ bookshop?

Megan: No, it hasn't. Go to Heffers. It's in the city centre. It's got millions of books!

Jamie: Don't buy books at a bookshop. Bookshops are very (2) _____ . Buy books on the Internet. They're very (3) _____ .

Paola: Has Cambridge got a good cinema?

Jamie: Yes, the Arts Cinema has got (4) _____ films.

Megan: No, it hasn't! Don't go there. The films are (5) _____! Go to the Multiplex. It's near the disco.

Mrs Williams: Take an umbrella. You're in England now! Here you are.

Paola: Thanks. Have you got a book about 'Where To Go' in Cambridge?

Mrs Williams: Yes, take this book. Visit the university colleges. Trinity and King's are (6) _____ . And go to the Fitzwilliam Museum. It's got very good paintings.

Gabriela: That's interesting.

Mrs Williams: And don't be late for dinner!

IMPERATIVES
Presentation

6 Look at the examples with your teacher.

Affirmative	Negative
Go to Heffers.	**Don't go** there.
Buy books on the Internet.	**Don't buy** books there.
Take an umbrella.	**Don't be** late.

🔲 Listen and repeat.

Practice

7 Write sentences.

Example
Don't go to that cinema. It's got terrible films.
Go to the Olympic cinema.

1 cinema/terrible films
2 café/good coffee
3 disco/terrible music
4 bookshop/interesting books
5 museum/fantastic paintings
6 market/cheap T-shirts

A – Z

8 Work in pairs. Student A is a tourist. Student B is from your area.

Example
A: *Has this town got a good bookshop?*
B: *Yes, it has. Go to _____ . It's got cheap books. Don't go to _____ . It's expensive.*

9 Look at the Key Words. Check the meaning.

KEY WORDS: Instructions

open/close your (books/bag)
write (a sentence/your name)
put your (pencil/pen/book) on the desk/floor
read (the dialogue on page 66)
look at (the teacher/your partner/the door/the window)
stand up/sit down

Write eight instructions for your partner.

Example
1 *Open your book on page ten.*
2 *Look at the photo.*
3 *Don't read the dialogue.*

Now work in pairs. Take turns to give your partner instructions and follow them.

10 🔲 Listen to the instructions. The last person to do an instruction is out of the game.

👉 Now do *Extra Time 9* on page 119.

10 In Town

Before you start

A–Z

1 🔘 Check the meaning of the Key Words. Listen and repeat.

KEY WORDS:

Food and Drink

sandwiches: cheese, egg, tomato
drinks: orange juice, mineral water, tea, coffee

---

2 What are your favourites?

Example
sandwiches – cheese sandwiches
drink – tea

3 🔘 Listen and repeat.

KEY WORDS: Shopping

CD, envelope, football shirt, magazine, newspaper, postcard, poster, stamp, T-shirt

---

Where are the objects from: a newsagent's, a market or both?

Example
newspaper – newsagent's

Reading and Listening

4 🔘 Read and listen. Match the dialogues (1, 2, 3) with the photos (A, B, C).

1
Kostas: A cheese sandwich, please.
Waitress: I'm sorry. We haven't got any cheese sandwiches. We've got some egg sandwiches.
Kostas: OK, an egg sandwich, please. And a coffee.
Adam: An orange juice for me, please.

2
Kostas: Have you got any big T-shirts?
Man: Yes, I have. Large or extra large?
Kostas: Large, please. And have you got any Manchester United football shirts?
Man: I'm sorry. I haven't.

3
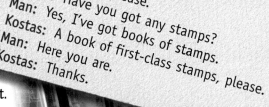
Adam: Some envelopes, please.
Man: Twenty or fifty?
Adam: Twenty, please.
Kostas: Have you got any stamps?
Man: Yes, I've got books of stamps.
Kostas: A book of first-class stamps, please.
Man: Here you are.
Kostas: Thanks.

A

some/any
Presentation

5 Look at the examples in the table with your teacher.

Affirmative

We've got **some** egg sandwiches.

Negative

We haven't got **any** cheese sandwiches.

Question

Have you got **any** stamps?

Short Answers

Yes, I have.   No, I haven't.

 Listen and repeat.

Practice

6 Write sentences about the list.

Example
We've got some mineral water. We haven't got any envelopes.

envelopes ✗	cheese ✓
mineral water ✓	tomatoes ✗
stamps ✗	coffee ✗
salad ✓	orange juice ✓
postcards ✗	tea ✗

7 Work in pairs. Look at the picture of the newsagent's. Ask and answer questions.

Example
A: *Have you got any magazines?*
B: *Yes, we have.*
A: *Have you got any T-shirts?*
B: *No, we haven't got any.*

8 Work in pairs. Act out the dialogues from Exercise 4. Ask for the things in the table.

Example
A: *A tomato sandwich, please.*
B: *I'm sorry. We haven't got any tomato sandwiches.*
A: *OK, a cheese sandwich, please. And a mineral water.*

	café	market	newsagent's
A	a tomato sandwich a mineral water	a small T-shirt a poster	postcards (5) a book of second-class stamps
B	an egg sandwich a coffee	a football shirt a CD	envelopes (50) two books of first-class stamps

☞ Now do *Extra Time 10* on page 119.

Communication Workshop

Writing: A Description of a Place

1 Read Adam's description of his city and area. Look at the sentences with *but*.

2 Use the cues to write sentences with *but*.

Example
The town has got a cinema **but** *it hasn't got a disco.*

1 cinema (+)/disco (–)
2 three cafés (+)/
   bookshops (–)
3 post office (+)/banks (–)
4 café (+)/hotels (–)

I am from Toruń in Poland. It is not very big <u>but</u> it is historic and very beautiful. Go to the main square. It has got a statue of Nicolaus Copernicus, the famous astronomer from our city. Toruń has got some very beautiful old houses and churches. Visit the church of St John's and the Town Hall. Toruń has got three or four good museums. Visit the Copernicus museum. It is very interesting.
The area near my house has got some shops. It has got two cafés <u>but</u> it hasn't got any hotels, banks or bookshops.

Write a description of your town. Follow the stages below.

Stage 1

Make notes about these things.

*   name of the place – big/small, old/modern, a good place to visit
*   other buildings/places to visit in the town/city
*   things in your local area

Stage 2

Use your notes to write a description of your town and area.

Talkback

Work in pairs. Compare your descriptions. Find differences.

Example
My area hasn't got a hotel but it has got a café.

Speaking: Asking about Places

Ask and answer questions about places. Follow the stages below.

Stage 1

Student A: read about the places near Paola's and Gabriela's house in Cambridge (on page 128).
Student B: read about the places near Adam's and Kostas's house (on page 128).

Stage 2

Work in pairs. Ask and answer questions about the places (shops/cinemas/discos/parks etc.)

Example
A: *Has Adam's and Kostas's area got any shops?*
B: *Yes, it has. It has got a supermarket and two ...*

Talkback

Which house is in the best area?

6 Playing sport

In this module you ...

- Talk about sports and times.
- Read and listen to dialogues.
- Read and complete a form.
- Learn about *can* and *there is/are*.

Warm-up

pages 18–19

1 🔊 Listen and repeat the Key Words.

KEY WORDS: Sports

athletics, basketball, diving, football, skiing, swimming, tennis

2 Match the Key Words with the pictures.

3 List your favourite things. Then complete the table for your partner.

	me
My favourite sport (to do)	basketball
My favourite sport on TV	tennis
My favourite sports star	André Agassi
My favourite team	Manchester United

	my partner
My favourite sport (to do)	
My favourite sport on TV	
My favourite sports star	
My favourite team	

Now work in pairs. Ask and answer questions.

Example
A: *What's your favourite sport?*
B: *Tennis.*

Tell the class about your partner.

1   2   3   4   5   6   7

11 My Favourite Sports

Kostas

Gabriela

Paola

Adam

Before you start

1 Look at the photos. What are their favourite sports?

Example
Kostas – diving

pages 18–19

2 Listen and repeat.

KEY WORDS: Sports

play football/basketball/tennis; ski; swim
Athletics: do the long jump/high jump; run the 100 metres; jump 3 metres

What sports are you good at?

Example
I am good at skiing.

Reading and Listening

3 Read and listen to the dialogue. What sports are Adam and Paola good at?

Adam: My favourite sports are football, basketball and athletics. What are your favourites, Paola?

Paola: Athletics. Running is my favourite. I can run the 100 metres in 14 seconds.

Adam: Wow! My favourite is the long jump. I can jump 3 metres.

Paola: Really? I can't jump very well! What other sports can you do?

Adam: Well, I can ski. And I can swim and play football. And you? Can you ski?

Paola: No, I can't. I can swim and I can play tennis but not very well!

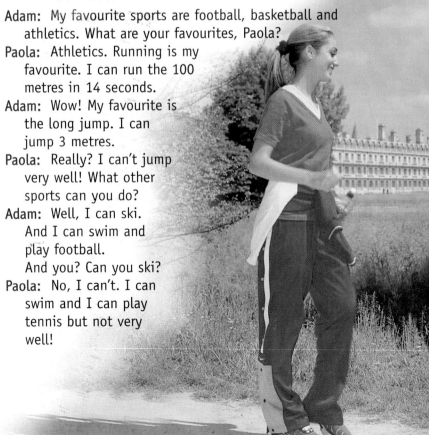

can/can't

Presentation

4 Look at the examples with your teacher. Listen and repeat.

Affirmative	I/You/He/She/It/ We/You/They	**can** swim.
Negative	I/You/He/She/It/ We/You/They	**cannot (can't)** jump.
Questions	**Can** I/you/he/she/it/ we/you/they	ski?
Short Answers	Yes, I/you/he/she/it/ we/you/they	**can.**
	No, I/you/he/she/it/ we/you/they	**can't.**

Practice

5 Look at the table below. Write ten sentences about Kostas and Gabriela.

Example
Gabriela can ski.

	Gabriela	Kostas	You
ski	✓	✗	No, I can't
swim	✓	✓	No, I can
dive	✗	✓	
play football	✓	✓	
play tennis	✓	✗	
play basketball	✓	✗	

6 Complete the table about you. Then work in pairs. Ask and answer questions.

Example
A: *Can you swim?*
B: *Yes, I can. Can you play tennis?*

A–Z

7 Read the Key Words. Look at the pictures and write sentences.

KEY WORDS: Adverbs

brilliantly, fast, well, very well, not very well

Example
1 *He can't play tennis very well!*

8 Work in pairs. Ask and answer questions. Use adverbs.

Example
A: *Can you run fast?*
B: *No, I can't. Can you swim well?*
A: *Yes, I can.*

☞ Now do *Extra Time 11* on page 120.

12 A Sports Centre

SPORTS CENTRE

Open 9.00 a.m. – 9.00 p.m.

Swimming pool
Open – 9.30 a.m. – 8.30 p.m.

Swimming classes
9.30, 10.30, 11.30 a.m.

Gym
Open 9.00 a.m. – 1.15 p.m./
2.00 p.m. – 8.30 p.m.

Aerobic classes
2.45, 3.45, 7.45 p.m.

Tennis courts
Open 9.00 a.m. – 8.00 p.m.

Tennis classes
4.00, 5.00, 6.00 p.m.

Olympic Café
Open 10.00 a.m. – 7.00 p.m.

Before you start

A–Z

1 🔊 Listen and repeat the Key Words.

KEY WORDS: Sports

basketball court, football pitch, gym, jacuzzi, sauna, (indoor) swimming pool, tennis court

Look at the information about the sports centre. What Key Words are not there?

Reading and Listening

2 🔊 Read and listen. Complete the dialogue with these adjectives.

big, boring, fantastic, good, great, new, terrible

Kostas: Megan, is there a sports centre near here?
Megan: Yes, there's a (1) _____ place near Newmarket Road. It's got a (2) _____ gym.
Kostas: (3) _____! Is there a swimming pool?
Megan: Yes, there are two pools. There's a children's pool and a (4) _____ pool.
Kostas: Good. There's a big pool near my house in Rhodes. And is there a sauna?
Megan: No, there isn't. And there isn't a jacuzzi. There are five tennis courts but there aren't indoor courts.
Kostas: Mmmm ... I can't play tennis very well. Are there tennis classes?
Megan: Yes, there are. There are tennis classes in the afternoon.
Kostas: Can you play tennis?
Megan: Not very well! I'm (5) _____!
Kostas: Well, come to the tennis classes with me!
Megan: That's a good idea, but ... I haven't got a good tennis racket.
Paola: I've got two tennis rackets. Take this racket. It's (6) _____ .
Jamie: Come on, Megan. Don't be (7) _____!
Megan: OK.

there is/there are
Presentation

3 Look at the examples with your teacher.

🔊 Listen and repeat.

Affirmative	
Singular	**There is (There's)** a children's pool.
Plural	**There are (There're)** two pools.
Negative	
Singular	**There is not (isn't)** a jacuzzi.
Plural	**There are not (aren't)** indoor courts.
Questions	
Singular	**Is there** a sports centre near here?
Plural	**Are there** tennis classes?
Short Answers		
Singular	Yes, **there is.**	No, **there isn't.**
Plural	Yes, **there are.**	No, **there aren't.**

Practice

4 Use the cues to write sentences.

Example
There isn't a basketball court in the sports centre.

1 a basketball court ✘   5 a gym ✔
2 a café ✔   6 a restaurant ✘
3 a football pitch ✘   7 two swimming pools ✔
4 a sauna ✘   8 five tennis courts ✔

Now work in pairs. Ask and answer questions about the places.

Example
A: *Is there a basketball court in the sports centre?*
B: *No, there isn't.*

5 Write sentences about your town or area. Use the words below.

sports centre, hotel, supermarket, café, post office, mosque, museum, disco, park, railway station, swimming pool

Example
There are two sports centres in my town.
There is one museum.

Now work in pairs. Ask and answer the questions about your town.

Example
A: *Is there a sports centre?*
B: *Yes, there are two.*

 **page 22**

6 🔊 Listen and repeat the times.

11.00 (eleven o'clock), 6.00 (six o'clock),
8.30 (eight thirty), 12.30 (twelve thirty),
7.15 (seven fifteen), 10.15 (ten fifteen),
9.45 (nine forty-five), 1.45 (one forty-five),
3.20 (three twenty), 6.25 (six twenty-five)

7 Work in pairs. Ask and tell the time.

Example
A: *What's the time?*
B: *It's nine o'clock.*

 *Prepositions* **at, in**

8 Look at the sentence. Write four sentences about today's classes.

Example
*English is **at** 10 o'clock **in** the morning.*

at five o'clock/ten o'clock, etc.
in the morning (a.m.)/
in the afternoon (⟶ 6 p.m.)/
in the evening (6 p.m. ⟶)

☞ Now do *Extra Time 12* on page 120.

43

Communication Workshop

Writing: Completing a Form

1 Match the information about Paola with the parts of the form.

a) Italian/French
b) Siena
c) Ms E. Austen
d) Italian
e) Paola
f) music/athletics
g) 16
h) Rossi
i) Class 6 C
j) swim/run 100 metres (in 14 seconds)
k) Miss
l) 9.30-13.00; 14.00-16.00

MILTON SCHOOL OF ENGLISH

Surname (1) _____

First name (2) _____

Title (Mr/Miss/Ms/Mrs) (3) _____

Age (4) _____   Nationality (5) _____

Home town (6) _____

Name of teacher (7) _____

Class (8) _____   Time of classes (9) _____

Interests (10) _____

Sports (11) _____

Languages (12) _____

---

2 Write the names below correctly.

Example
1 *Mr S.F. Jones*

1 mr sf jones
2 ms ga edwards
3 mr ml thomas   4 mrs er hanlon
5 miss b smith   6 mr rdt brown

Complete the form with information about you. Follow the stages below.

Stage 1
Read the form. Write your answers on a piece of paper.

Stage 2
Check your answers for spelling and punctuation.

Stage 3
Now copy and complete the form.

Speaking: Personal Information

Find out and give information. Follow the stages below.

Stage 1
Write questions for the form. Practise saying the questions.

Example
What classes are you in?
What languages can you speak?

Stage 2
Work in pairs. Ask and answer your questions. Include one piece of false information in your answers.

Review

Grammar

1 Use the verbs to write imperatives about your English classroom.

1 run 2 listen to the teacher 3 eat food
4 play football 5 speak English
6 speak your language 7 use the Mini-dictionary
8 drink coffee 9 ask questions
10 listen to music 11 use your vocabulary book

Example
Don't run in the classroom. Listen to the teacher in lessons.

2 Look at the teacher's list. Write questions and answers.

Example
Have we got any pencils? Yes, we have.

3 Correct these sentences about your classroom.

1 There are two boards.
2 There is a bed in the classroom.
3 There are ten desks.
4 There are fifteen windows.
5 There are two big sofas.
6 There is a computer on my desk.

Vocabulary

4 Find the place words.

Example
1 *park*

1 karp 2 waylair niotast 3 reriv 4 chchru
5 nami rauesq 6 teksupmarre 7 oookbshp

5 Write down the times.

Example
1 *six o'clock in the morning*

1 6.00 a.m.
2 2.15 p.m.
3 11.30 a.m.
4 7.45 a.m.
5 4.00 p.m.
6 1.30 p.m.
7 10.45 a.m.
8 3.15 p.m.

6 Complete the words.

Example
1 *post office*

1 post _____
2 mineral _____
3 high _____
4 railway _____
5 sports _____
6 orange _____
7 swimming _____
8 tennis _____

Pronunciation

7 🔊 Listen to the two sounds.

a) s<u>h</u>ip /ʃ/ b) <u>ch</u>ips /tʃ/

Write a or b for the <u>underlined</u> sounds.

Example 1 *a*

1 s<u>h</u>e   2 book<u>sh</u>op
3 <u>ch</u>eese   4 dic<u>ti</u>onary   5 <u>ch</u>eck
6 Ru<u>ss</u>ian   7 <u>ch</u>urch   8 Briti<u>sh</u>
9 na<u>ti</u>onality   10 <u>ch</u>ildren

🔊 Listen and repeat.

Culture Corner 3

CAMBRIDGE FACTFILE

POPULATION – 105,000

LOCATION – LONDON 80 KM

Places to see

CHURCHES
Saint Benet (Saxon)
King's College Chapel

UNIVERSITY COLLEGES
King's College
St John's College
Queens' College
Trinity College

PARKS AND RIVER CAM

MUSEUMS
Fitzwilliam Museum
(art/history)
Cambridge Museum

FAMOUS EX-STUDENTS FROM CAMBRIDGE UNIVERSITY
scientists – Isaac Newton /
    Charles Darwin
poet – John Milton
politician – Oliver Cromwell
    (head of the English
    Republic: 1651–59)

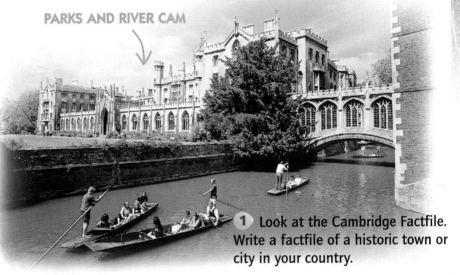

1 Look at the Cambridge Factfile.
Write a factfile of a historic town or
city in your country.

Learning Power!

Classroom Language

1 🔊 Listen and order the classroom instructions.

a) Match the Key Words with the photos.
b) Listen and repeat the words.
c) Work in pairs.
d) Read and listen to the dialogue.
e) Write five sentences about your family.
f) Ask and answer questions.
g) Complete the table with these words.
h) Work in groups.
i) Listen and complete the dialogue.

2 🔊 Listen and complete the sentences.

1 Can I open a _____ , please?
2 Can I go to the _____ , please?
3 Have you got a _____ ?
4 Can we use a _____ ?

🔊 Listen again and repeat the sentences.

A

B

C

7 Every day

In this module you...

- **Read** descriptions of routines.
- **Read** and **listen to** dialogues.
- **Talk about** your routines.
- **Write about** your school day.
- **Learn about** the *Present Simple* tense.

Warm-up

 page 23

1 Write the days of the week in the correct order.

KEY WORDS: Days

Tuesday, Sunday, Friday, Monday, Thursday, Saturday, Wednesday

🔊 Listen and check your answers. Repeat the words.

2 Match the captions (1–4) with the photos (A–D).

1 Shopping on Saturday.
2 Monday morning again!
3 An English Sunday lunch.
4 Friday night at the cinema.

3 Work in pairs. Ask and answer the questions.

1 What is your favourite day of the week?
2 What days have you got science lessons?
3 When is your favourite TV programme?
4 What day is your birthday this year?

D

13 Weekends

Before you start

A–Z

1 🔊 Listen and repeat the Key Words.

KEY WORDS: Routines

do the shopping/your homework, get up early, go out,
go swimming, go to class/the city centre/the cinema/
a disco/the Internet café, have breakfast/lunch,
meet friends, read the newspaper, watch TV

Reading and Listening

2 🔊 Read and listen. Complete the dialogue with Key Words.

Gabriela: It's the weekend!

Megan: Yes, no school for two days. On Fridays I watch TV or
I (1) _____ .

Paola: With Jamie?

Megan: No, with my friends. (*to Jamie*) You
(2) _____ every Friday. That's boring.

Jamie: No, it isn't!

Gabriela: And on Saturdays?

Megan: My dad and I go to the sports centre in the morning.
We (3) _____ .

Paola: Ah, you go swimming. Great!

Megan: I have lunch with my parents and in the afternoon
they (4) _____ .
I (5) _____ or a disco on Saturday nights.

Gabriela: Great! I go to discos in Argentina.

PRESENT SIMPLE: AFFIRMATIVE (*I, you, we, they*) Presentation

3 Look at the examples with your teacher.

Affirmative

I **go** to the city centre.

You **go** to the Internet café.

We **go** swimming.

You **go** swimming.

They **do** the shopping.

🔊 Listen and repeat the examples.

Practice

4 Write true sentences with times and days.

1 I do English homework on ~~Saturday~~ .
2 My parents do the shopping on _____ .
3 I get up at _____ on _____ .
4 I watch my favourite TV programme on

_____ .

5 My parents go to bed at _____ .
6 I play sport every _____ .

5 Complete the text with the verbs.

meet, play, go (x2), have, get up, do

On Monday morning I (1) ~~get up~~ at
7 o'clock. I (2) ~~have~~ a big breakfast.
I (3) _____ to school at 8 o'clock on the
bus. Some of my friends (4) _____
their homework on the bus! At school,
I (5) _____ my friends and we
(6) _____ basketball. At 9 o'clock we
(7) _____ to our class.

Reading and Listening

6 🔊 Read and listen. Put these in order (1–4).

have lunch ☐ do homework ☐ meet friends ☐
get up ☐

Megan: We don't get up early on Sundays.
Jamie: Well, you don't get up early, Megan.
Megan: OK, Jamie. I don't have breakfast – we
have a big Sunday lunch. Our parents read
the newspapers – they don't go out. I meet
my friends in the afternoon.
Gabriela: You two don't have busy weekends.
Megan: And on Sunday evening I do my
homework.
Gabriela: Oh, no! Homework! Jamie, have you
got a CD encyclopedia?

PRESENT SIMPLE: NEGATIVE
(*I, you, we, they*)
Presentation

7 Look at the examples with your teacher.

> **Negative**
>
> I **don't have** breakfast.
>
> You **don't get up** early.
>
> We **don't get up** early.
>
> You **don't have** busy weekends.
>
> They **don't go** out.

🔊 Listen and repeat the examples.

Practice

8 Write three affirmative sentences and three
negative sentences about *you*. Include one false
sentence. Use the Key Words from Exercise 1.

Example
*I get up for school at 7.30. I don't watch TV on
Saturdays.*

Now work in pairs. Read your sentences to your
partner. He/She guesses the false information.

Prepositions **on, in**

9 Look at the examples from the dialogue.

*I watch TV **on** Fridays.*
*They do the shopping **in** the afternoon.*

Complete the sentences with *on* or *in*.

1 I get up early _on_ Saturdays.
2 I do my homework _in_ the evening.
3 We have English homework _on_ Wednesdays.
4 I play tennis _on_ Tuesdays and Thursdays.
5 _on_ Saturdays, we do the shopping
_in_ the morning.
6 _in_ the evening, I go to the cinema.

☛ Now do *Extra Time 13* on page 120.

14 Routines

Kostas's mother works at home. She translates English texts into Greek. She gets up early and she makes breakfast. Then she cleans the house. She does the shopping and then works in the afternoon.

Before you start

1 Listen and repeat the Key Words.

> **KEY WORDS: Routines**
>
> clean the house, make breakfast, meet people, play the guitar, study, travel

Reading and Listening

2 Read and listen to the texts. Match the people with their jobs.

businesswoman, computer programmer, doctor, student, translator

PRESENT SIMPLE: AFFIRMATIVE (*he, she, it*)
Presentation

3 Look at the examples with your teacher.

> **Affirmative**
>
> He works in a clinic.
> She goes to university.
> She studies in the evening.
> She plays the guitar.
> It sleeps near her computer.

Listen and repeat the examples.

4 Pronunciation. Listen and repeat these verbs.

1 make, makes; visit, visits; work, works; write, writes
2 clean, cleans; go, goes; play, plays; read, reads; study, studies
3 dance, dances; teach, teaches; watch, watches

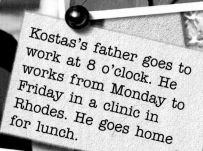

Kostas's father goes to work at 8 o'clock. He works from Monday to Friday in a clinic in Rhodes. He goes home for lunch.

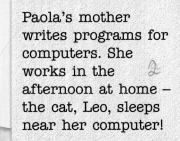

Paola's mother writes programs for computers. She works in the afternoon at home – the cat, Leo, sleeps near her computer!

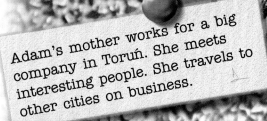

Adam's mother works for a big company in Toruń. She meets interesting people. She travels to other cities on business.

Gabriela's sister goes to university in the morning. She has lunch in the university coffee bar – she has a sandwich or burger and fruit juice. She studies in the evening. In her free time she plays the guitar in a group.

Practice

5 Write sentences in the Present Simple.

1 Megan _lives_ (live) in Cambridge.
2 Her mother _works_ (work) in an office.
3 Her father _teaches_ (teach) sport.
4 Adam _watches_ (watch) football every week.
5 His brother _studies_ (study) medicine at university.
6 Gabriela _goes_ (go) to bed late.
7 Paola _plays_ (play) the piano.
8 Kostas _paints_ (paint) in his free time.

6 Write five sentences about your family and friends. Use the verbs in Exercise 4.

Example
My sister goes to university.

PRESENT SIMPLE: NEGATIVE (*he, she, it*)
Presentation

7 Look at the examples with your teacher.

Negative

He **doesn't work** on Saturdays and Sundays.
She **doesn't go** out to work.
She **doesn't study** at weekends.
She **doesn't go** home for lunch.
It **doesn't sleep** at night.

Listen and repeat the examples.

Who are *he*, *she* and *it* in the examples?

Gabriela's sister, Kostas's mother, Kostas's father, Paola's cat

Listen and check your answers.

8 Complete the sentences in the Present Simple.

1 Adam's mother _doesn't work_ (not work) for a small company.
2 Adam _doesn't play_ (not play) the piano.
3 Gabriela _doesn't go_ (not go) to bed early.
4 Gabriela's sister _____ (not go) home for lunch.
5 Kostas _____ (not drink) Coke.
6 Kostas's mother _doesn't get up_ (not get up) late.

9 Complete the text with the verbs in the Present Simple.

My mother is a teacher at my school and my father (1) _works_ (work) in a bank. He (2) _gets up_ (get up) at 6.30. He (3) _doesn't have_ (not have) breakfast. He (4) _reads_ (read) the morning newspaper and (5) _has_ (have) a cup of coffee. My mother and I (6) _get up_ (get up) at 7 o'clock and she (7) _makes_ (make) our breakfast. I (8) _have_ (have) a shower and I (9) _clean_ (clean) my teeth. I (10) _don't watch_ (not watch) breakfast TV. My mum (11) _listens_ (listen) to music on the radio. My father (12) _goes_ (go) to work at 7.45 – he (13) _takes_ (take) our car. My mum (14) _doesn't go_ (not go) with him – we (15) _walk_ (walk) to the bus stop at 8.30.

Now do *Extra Time 14* on page 120.

51

Communication Workshop

Writing: My School Day

1 Read the text. Are these sentences true (T) or false (F)?

1 Paola has orange juice for breakfast.
2 She goes to school on a bus.
3 There are five hours of lessons every day.
4 She watches TV in the evening.

2 Look at these sentences.

Kostas's mother gets up early and she makes breakfast. **Then** she cleans the house. She does the shopping and **then** works in the afternoon.

Complete the text with *and*, *but* or *then*.

My School Day, by Paola

I get up at 7 o'clock. I have breakfast – milk and biscuits. (1) _____ I have a shower (2) _____ I clean my teeth. I walk to school. At school, I talk with my friends. (3) _____ the teacher comes (4) _____ we go to our class. In the morning, lessons are 8 o'clock to 1 o'clock. (5) _____ I go to the café with my friends. We eat (6) _____ talk. In the afternoon, there aren't any lessons. We have school on Saturdays (7) _____ we don't have school on Sundays. After lunch, I go home (8) _____ I do my homework. (9) _____ I play the piano – that's my hobby. We eat at 8 o'clock. I don't watch TV (10) _____ I watch videos. I go to bed at 10.30.

Write about your school day. Follow the stages.

Stage 1

Write notes for before, during and after school.

Example

> Before School
> have shower
> have breakfast
> clean teeth

Stage 2

Write sentences about your school day. Join sentences with *and*, *but* and *then*.

Stage 3

Divide your writing into *three* paragraphs:

- before school
- at school
- after school

Stage 4

Check your work for:
punctuation ✓ Present Simple tense ✓ spelling ✓

Speaking: Guess the Student

Play a guessing game about your routines. Follow the stages.

Stage 1

Work in groups. Read the descriptions of your school days. Write down two things each student does. *Don't* write their name.

Example
This person listens to the radio in the morning.

Stage 2

Take turns to read out sentences. The others guess who it is. Don't speak if the answer is you!

Example
A: *This person has fruit for breakfast.*
B: *Carol?*
A: *No.*
C: *Sandra?*
A: *Yes!*

1
2
3
4
5

8 Free time

In this module you ...

- **Talk about** your free time and do a survey.
- **Read** a letter and **listen to** dialogues.
- **Write** a letter.
- **Learn about** Present Simple Questions, and 'likes' and 'dislikes'.

Warm-up

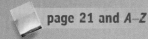

page 21 and *A–Z*

1 🔘 Listen and repeat the Key Words.

> **KEY WORDS: Free Time**
>
> collect things,
> go dancing/fishing/swimming/to the cinema,
> listen to music/CDs,
> play computer games/football/the piano,
> read books, surf the Internet, take photos,
> watch videos/television/sport

2 What free time activities can you see in the photos?

3 Write three sentences about your hobbies and free time activities.

Example
On Saturdays I surf the Internet at the Internet café.

Now tell the class about your free time.

Example
I go fishing with my dad every weekend.

6

7

15 Relaxing

Before you start

 page 23

1 ▢⊙ **Listen and repeat the Key Words.**

KEY WORDS: Frequency

once a week/month,
twice a week/month,
three times a week/month,
every day/week/month

Now use the Key Words to tell the class how often you do things.

Examples
I go to the cinema once a week, on Fridays.
I play tennis twice a week, on Tuesdays and Thursdays.
I listen to music every day.

Reading and Listening

2 ▢⊙ **Read and listen to Gabriela and Adam. Complete the gaps.**

Gabriela: What do you do in your free time in Poland?
Adam: Well, I play football for my school.
Gabriela: How often do you play?
Adam: We play once a week, on (1) _____.
Gabriela: Do you play other sports?
Adam: Yes, I do, I play (2) _____ with my brother.
Gabriela: Does he go to your school?
Adam: No, he doesn't. He goes to university. Do you play sports?
Gabriela: No, I don't.
Adam: What do you do in your free time?
Gabriela: I go to the (3) _____ .
Adam: Does it finish late?
Gabriela: Yes, about midnight.
Adam: How often do you go?
Gabriela: Oh, twice a week, on (4) _____ and Saturdays, with my sister.
Adam: Does she go to university?
Gabriela: Yes, she does.
Adam: Do you have other hobbies?
Gabriela: Well, I go shopping – that's my hobby!
Adam: You're crazy! Do you like films?
Gabriela: Yes, I do.
Adam: Er, do you want to go to the (5) _____ tonight?

PRESENT SIMPLE: *Yes/No* QUESTIONS
Presentation

3 🔊 Look at the examples with your teacher. Listen and repeat.

'Yes/No' Questions

Do	I/you/we/they	play	sports?
Does	he/she	go	to university?
Does	it	finish	late?

Short Answers

Yes,		**do.**
	I/you/we/they	
No,		**don't.**
Yes,		**does.**
	he/she/it	
No,		**doesn't.**

Practice

4 Write *Yes/No* questions.

Example
Do you play football for your school?

1 you play football for your school?
2 they go fishing?
3 she go to the cinema every weekend?
4 he surf the Internet?
5 you listen to music every day?

🔊 Listen and check your answers. Repeat the questions.

5 Work in pairs. Look at the Key Words on page 53. Ask and answer questions.

Example
A: *Do you collect things?*
B: *Yes, I do. I collect stamps. Do you go fishing?*
A: *No, I don't.*

PRESENT SIMPLE: *Wh-* QUESTIONS
Presentation

6 🔊 Look at the examples with your teacher. Listen and repeat.

Wh- Questions

What When	**do**	I/you/we/they	
How often Where	**does**	he/she/it	play?

Practice

7 Write *Wh-* questions.

Example
1 *What sport do you play?*

1 what/sport/you play?
2 how often/you go to the cinema?
3 where/he play football?
4 when/they go swimming?
5 how often/she go dancing?

🔊 Listen and check your answers. Repeat the questions.

8 Use the cues to write questions.

Computers	how often?/surf the Internet?/what CD games?
A sport	play a sport?/how often?/where?
Dancing	how often?/when?/where?/go to discos?

Example
How often do you use a computer?

Now work in pairs. Ask your partner your questions.

Example
A: *How often do you use a computer?*
B: *Every day.*
A: *Do you surf the Internet?*
B: *No, I don't. I haven't got the Internet.*

☞ Now do *Extra Time 15* on page 121.

16 At the Cinema

Before you start

1 Match the British prices (1–5) with how you say them (a–e).

1 £2.50   a) one pound ninety-nine
2 75p   b) two pounds fifty
3 £1.99   c) four pounds twenty-five
4 £4.25   d) ten 'p'
5 10p   e) seventy-five 'p'

 Listen and check your answers. Repeat the prices.

A–Z

2 Listen and repeat the Key Words.

KEY WORDS: Films
action films, comedy films, science fiction films, westerns

What films do you like?

Reading and Listening

3 Read and listen to the dialogue and complete it with the Key Words from Exercise 2.

Adam: I love going to the cinema. I go every week.
Gabriela: Me, too. I like (1) _____ but I hate (2) _____ .
Adam: Here we are. What do you want to see?
Gabriela: Er, well, not the new 'Star Wars'. I don't like (3) _____ .
Adam: Hey, the new Schwarzenegger film is on.
Gabriela: No, I hate (4) _____ . Do you like Sandra Bullock?
Adam: Yes, she's really good.
Gabriela: OK. How much is it?
Adam: Four pounds fifty.
Gabriela: Right. And then we can go to a disco – you know I love discos!

like/don't like
Presentation

4 Look at the examples with your teacher.

I love football!   I like football.

I don't like football.   I hate football!

 Listen and repeat the examples.

5 Look at these sentences.

Subject/verb	+ noun
I love	discos.
I don't like	science fiction films.
Do you like	Sandra Bullock?

Subject/verb	+ -ing
I love	dan**cing**.
I don't like	watch**ing** science fiction films.
Do you like	go**ing** to the cinema?

Find similar sentences in the dialogue in Exercise 3.

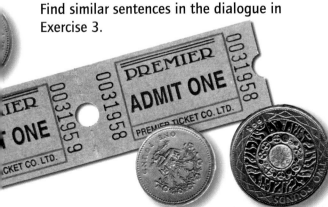

Practice

6 Do you like these things? Write six sentences. Use *love, like, don't like* or *hate.*

Coke, dancing, football, mathematics, reading, science fiction films

7 Complete this survey.

A: Can I ask you some questions? Do you like action films?
B: Yes, they're great! I (1) _____ action films.
A: Do you like the food here in England?
B: It's OK.
A: Really? My friends think it's horrible – they (2) _____ English food. Next question. Do you like Ricky Martin?
B: No, I (3) _____ Latin music. I (4) _____ heavy metal music.

 Listen and check your answers.

8 Write five questions about the cinema.

Examples
Do you like westerns?
Do you like Nicole Kidman?

Now work in pairs. Ask and answer your questions.

Example
A: *Do you like westerns?*
B: *No, I don't like westerns. And you?*
A: *I love westerns.*

Prepositions **to**

9 Look at the examples. Then complete the sentences with *to, to the* or no preposition.

Examples
*I go fishing every week. I go **to** school on the bus. I go **to the** coffee bar for lunch.*

1 Do you want to go _____ cinema?
2 I go _____ bed at 10.30.
3 He goes _____ home for lunch.
4 We go _____ sports centre for tennis classes.
5 She goes _____ dancing every Friday.
6 My brother goes _____ university.

☞ Now do *Extra Time 16* on page 121.

Communication Workshop

Writing: A Letter

1 Read the letter to a penfriend. Match the paragraphs with these topics.

a) goodbye b) likes and dislikes c) family and pets

Dear Kurt,

(1) My name is Eva. I'm from Spain. I'm fifteen years old. My mother is a teacher and my father is a lawyer. I've got a brother called Pedro and I've got a dog called Niki.

(2) I love shopping. My favourite model is Inés Sastre from Spain. I also like dancing. At the weekend I go to a disco near my house. I like salsa music. My favourite singer is Ricky Martin. I hate heavy metal music! Do you like heavy metal music?

(3) Please write to me and tell me about the things you like.

Write soon!

Eva.

Write a letter to a penfriend. Follow the stages.

Stage 1

Write notes about these things.

Stage 2

Write your letter.

Stage 3

Check your letter for:
capital letters ✓ apostrophes ✓ full stops ✓

Talkback

In groups, read your letters. Do you like similar things?

Speaking: A Survey

Do a survey about hobbies and free time activities. Follow the stages.

Stage 1

Choose one topic and write three questions for a survey.
cinema/sport/music/hobbies

Example
Cinema
How often do you go to the cinema?
What films do you like?
Who is your favourite actor or actress?

Stage 2

Ask the other students your questions and write down the results.

Stage 3

Tell the class one result of your survey.

Example
Action films are very popular.

Review

Grammar

1 Complete the sentences with the verbs in the Present Simple.

1 My mother _____ (work) in a bank.
2 I _____ (listen) to the radio every morning.
3 What _____ (you/have) for breakfast?
4 He _____ (not play) the piano.
5 _____ (they/get up) early on Sundays?
6 She _____ (love) dancing but she _____ (not like) heavy metal music.
7 We _____ (not go) to school on the bus.
8 Where _____ (he/play) tennis?
9 She _____ (have) lunch at home every day.
10 _____ (he/read) the Sunday newspapers?

2 Put the words in the correct order to make questions.

1 you/do/like football?
2 he/does/play?/what
3 live?/they/do/where
4 she/go/does/to university?
5 finish/does/early?/it
6 do/they/go out?/when

3 Memory Game. Work in groups. Say true sentences using *love, like, don't like* and *hate*. If you can't remember, you are out of the game.

Example
Peter: *I like action films.*
Linda: *Peter likes action films. I love swimming.*
Tommy: *Peter likes action films, Linda loves swimming. I hate football.*
Vicky: *Peter likes action films, Linda loves swimming, Tommy hates football. I like dancing.*

Vocabulary

4 Match the verbs and the activities.

1	do	a)	breakfast
2	have	b)	a magazine
3	go	c)	the shopping
4	meet	d)	the Internet
5	play	e)	a friend
6	read	f)	swimming
7	surf	g)	television
8	watch	h)	the piano

5 What does Fred do in his free time? Write sentences.

6 Put these in order of frequency:

every Saturday, every day, twice a month, three times a week, every month

7 Write these prices in words.

£3.50 / £6.99 / 50p / £12.75 / 20p

Pronunciation

8 🔊 Listen and repeat the words.

1 /æ/ bank, piano, sandwich, stamps, taxi
2 /ɑː/ can't, half, park, past, tomato

9 🔊 Now listen and repeat the sentences.

1 It's half past ten.
2 A cheese and tomato sandwich, please.
3 He can't play the piano.

Culture Corner 4

TEENAGERS IN BRITAIN: FACTFILE

Mobile Phones

85% of teenagers aged 13-16 have a mobile phone.
They spend about £15 a month on phone calls.

Money

The average 14-16 year-old receives £600 a year in pocket money and money from part-time jobs.

The Internet

One in four teenagers regularly use the Internet.

Television

Boys watch TV for 19 hours a week; girls watch it 16 hours per week.
The favourite TV programme for boys and girls is *Friends*.

Cinema

38% of boys like action films.
23% of girls like comedy films.

* Information from a 1998 survey.

1 Read the factfile. Write a similar factfile about students in your class.

Learning Power!

Studying

1 Look at these ideas for learning new words.

- Look at your vocabulary book every week – at home, at lunch or on the bus!
- Test yourself. Don't look at the definitions. Cover them with a piece of paper.
- Ask a friend to test you. Then test your friend.

2 Look at these ideas for doing homework.

- Do your homework in a quiet room.
- Decide how long you want to spend on the work – half an hour, an hour?
- Get ready. Make sure you have your pen, coursebook, vocabulary book and a dictionary.

9 Excursions

In this module you...

- Talk about situations and places.
- Read and listen to dialogues.
- Read and write about tourist information.
- Learn about the Present Continuous.

Warm-up

page 20

1 🔊 Listen and repeat the Key Words.

KEY WORDS: Places

art gallery, beach, castle, market, museum, nature reserve

What places can you see in the photos?

2 Work in pairs. Ask and answer the questions.

1 Do you go on trips with your school? Where do you go?
2 Where do you go with your family?
3 Where do you like going? What places do you not like?

pages 12–13

3 🔊 Listen and repeat the Key Words.

KEY WORDS: Transport

by bus, by car, by coach, by plane, by train, by taxi, on foot

4 How do you travel? Complete the sentences.

Example
I go to school by bus.

1 I go to school _____ .
2 I go to the city centre _____ .
3 We go on school trips _____ .
4 We go on holiday _____ .

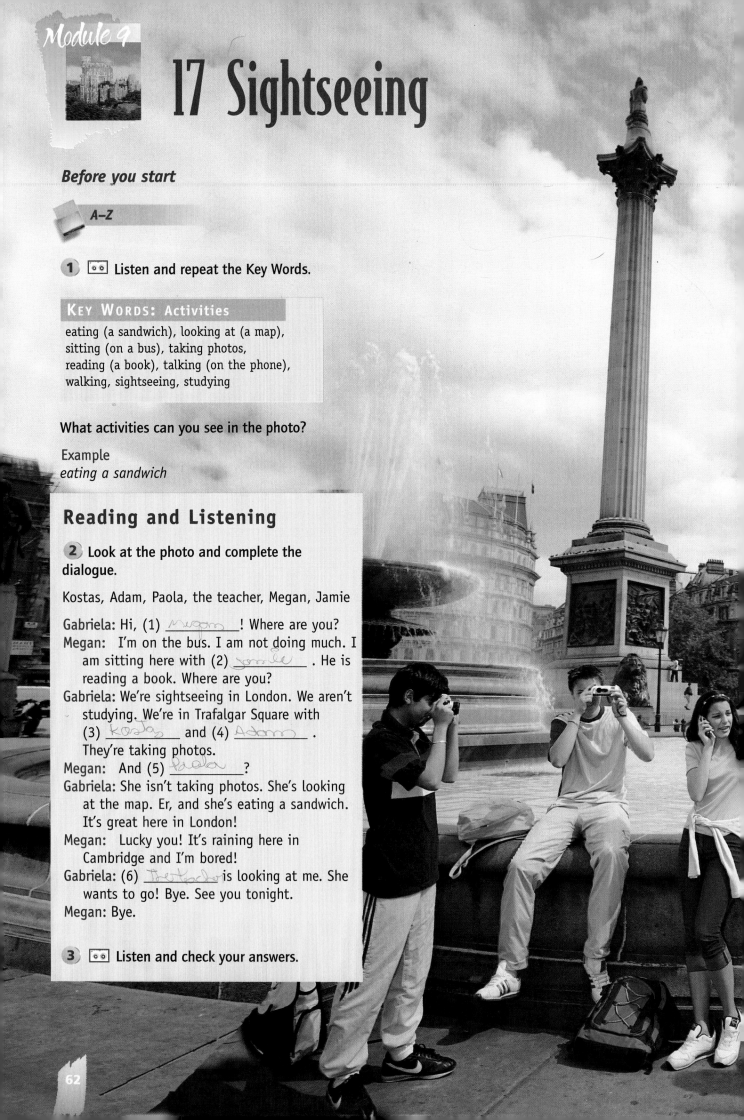

Module 9

17 Sightseeing

Before you start

A–Z

1 🔊 Listen and repeat the Key Words.

KEY WORDS: Activities

eating (a sandwich), looking at (a map),
sitting (on a bus), taking photos,
reading (a book), talking (on the phone),
walking, sightseeing, studying

What activities can you see in the photo?

Example
eating a sandwich

Reading and Listening

2 Look at the photo and complete the dialogue.

Kostas, Adam, Paola, the teacher, Megan, Jamie

Gabriela: Hi, (1) _Megan_! Where are you?

Megan:　I'm on the bus. I am not doing much. I am sitting here with (2) _Jamie_ . He is reading a book. Where are you?

Gabriela: We're sightseeing in London. We aren't studying. We're in Trafalgar Square with (3) _Kostas_ and (4) _Adam_ . They're taking photos.

Megan:　And (5) _Paola_ ?

Gabriela: She isn't taking photos. She's looking at the map. Er, and she's eating a sandwich. It's great here in London!

Megan:　Lucky you! It's raining here in Cambridge and I'm bored!

Gabriela: (6) _the teacher_ is looking at me. She wants to go! Bye. See you tonight.

Megan: Bye.

3 🔊 Listen and check your answers.

PRESENT CONTINUOUS:
AFFIRMATIVE/NEGATIVE
Presentation

4 Look at the examples with your teacher.

Affirmative		
I	am ('m)	
You/We/You/They	are ('re)	**taking** photos.
He/She	is ('s)	
It	is ('s)	**raining**.
Negative		
I	am not ('m not)	
You/We/You/They	are not (aren't)	**studying**.
He/She	is not (isn't)	
It	is not (isn't)	**raining**.

[°°] Listen and repeat.

Practice

5 Correct the information.

Example 1 *Gabriela and Megan are talking on the phone.*

1 Gabriela and Paola are talking on the phone.
2 Gabriela, Megan, Paola and Jamie are sightseeing in London.
3 Megan isn't sitting on a bus.
4 Jamie is watching television.
5 Adam and Kostas are looking at a map.
6 Paola is eating an orange.
7 It is raining in London.
8 Adam is looking at Gabriela.

6 Put the verbs in the dialogue in the correct form.

Megan: Hi, Gabi! Where are you now?
Gabriela: We're in the British museum. We (1) _____ (look) at some Egyptian statues. Paola (2) _____ (read) the guidebook. Kostas (3) _____ (not take) photos! He's with Adam. They (4) _____ (talk) to the teacher. Where are you?
Megan: I'm at home. I (5) _____ (do) my homework and I (6) _____ (listen) to music.
Gabriela: Where's Jamie?
Megan: Jamie and Mum aren't here. They (7) _____ (do) the shopping. Dad's in the garden. It (8) _____ (not rain) now.
Gabriela: Megan! Adam (9) _____ (not talk) to the teacher now. He's with that girl.
Megan: What girl?
Gabriela: Monique. She's French. They (10) _____ (look at) me!
Megan: Oh, sorry, Gabi. Mum's back. She (11) _____ (ask) for help. Bye!
Gabriela: Bye.

7 Imagine two situations.

a) You are at home with your family.
b) You are sightseeing in London with your friends.

Write sentences.

Example
a) *I'm in my bedroom. I'm reading. My sister's listening to music.*
b) *We're looking at Buckingham Palace. My friends are taking photos.*

8 Now work in pairs. You are on the phone. Ask and answer questions.

A: *Where are you?*
B: *I'm at home. I'm doing my homework. My dad's helping me with maths. And you?*

☞ Now do *Extra Time 17* on page 121.

18 Looking at Photos

Before you start

page 25

1 [cassette] Listen and repeat the Key Words.

KEY WORDS: CLOTHES

hat, jeans, jumper, shirt, shoes, shorts, skirt, T-shirt

What clothes can you see in the photo?

Example
Paola's wearing a shirt and jeans.
What clothes can't you see?

Reading and Listening

2 [cassette] Read and listen. Complete the dialogue with some of the Key Words.

Adam: This is a photo of a party at my school.
Gabriela: Who are you dancing with, Adam? She's wearing a nice red (1) _skirt_ . SkirT
Adam: A friend.
Paola: You're dancing very near to her. Are you kissing her?
Adam: No, I'm not! And in this photo...
Kostas: What are you doing? You're wearing a (2) _hat_ .
Adam: It's cold. We're visiting a nature reserve near my city.
Kostas: Is it snowing ... or is it your photography?
Adam: Yes, it is snowing. And in this photo we're on the bus...
Gabriela: Where are you going? You're wearing a
    (3) _shirt_ and (4) _shorts_ . Are you going to the beach?
    Shorts
Adam: Yes, we are.
Paola: Look – there's your 'friend' again, Adam. She's looking at you!!!
Adam: That's it. Show me your photos now, Paola!

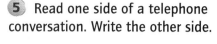

PRESENT CONTINUOUS: QUESTIONS
Presentation

3 🔲 Look at the examples with your teacher. Listen and repeat.

'Yes/No' Questions		
Am	I	
Are	you/we/they	**going** to the beach?
Is	he/she/it	
Short Answers		
	I	**am.**
Yes,	you/we/they	**are.**
	he/she/it	**is.**
	I	**am not ('m not).**
No,	you/we/they	**are not (aren't).**
	he/she/it	**is not (isn't).**
Wh- Questions		
	am	I
What	**are**	you/we/they	**doing?**
	is	he/she/it

Practice

4 Order the words to write questions. Add capital letters and punctuation.

Example
1 *Is Tim wearing a jumper?*

1 a jumper/Tim/wearing/is
2 Lucy/is/what/wearing
3 wearing/jeans/is/Lucy
4 is/what/wearing/ Sophie
5 T-shirts/wearing/are/ Tim and Lucy
6 Sophie/jeans/is/wearing

Write two more questions about the drawing.

Now work in pairs. Ask and answer the questions.

Example
A: *Is Tim wearing a jumper?*
B: *Yes, he is.*

5 Read one side of a telephone conversation. Write the other side.

Example
1 *What are you doing?*

A: (1 do) _____ ?
B: I'm sitting at home – doing my homework.
A: (2 study) _____ ?
B: No, I'm not studying English. I'm studying maths and listening to music.
A: (3 listen) _____ ?
B: I'm listening to Beck. He's great.
A: (4 do) _____ ?
B: My sister's watching TV.
A: (watch) _____ ?
B: She's watching an old film – starring Sean Connery.

6 Work in pairs. 'Phone' your partner. Ask and answer questions about your family.

Example
A: *Hi, it's me. What are you doing?*
B: *I'm reading a book about Egypt.*
A: *What's your brother doing?*

Prepositions **at, in, on**

7 Look at the prepositions.

*I'm **at** home in my bedroom. I'm sightseeing **in** London. We're **on** a bus.*

Complete the sentences with *at, in* and *on*.

1 We are sitting _on_ a train. We are _in_ London.
2 I am _at_ school _in_ the classroom.
3 She is _at_ home _in_ her bedroom.
4 They are _in_ a café having a drink.
5 He is _in_ bed reading a book.

👉 Now do *Extra Time 18* on page 121.

Communication Workshop

Writing: Tourist Information

1 Read Kostas's description. Replace *nice* with these adjectives to make the description interesting.

modern, fantastic, ancient, great, interesting, magnificent

2 Read the tourist information. Plan a weekend in Rhodes.

Example
Friday evening – walk around the streets/visit the old town

> **Write tourist information of a place to visit in your country. Follow the stages below.**

Stage 1
Choose a place. Make a list of interesting places to visit and excursions.

Stage 2
Write notes about each place.

Stage 3
Use your notes to write the information about the places.

Example
Visit the eight old hostels in the old town.

Talkback
Give your composition to your partner. Check your partner's information.

In the city
* Walk around the (1) <u>nice</u> streets. Go to the old town and see the eight old hostels or 'Inns' of the Knights of St John.
* Visit the 'Castello' or Palace of the Grand Master of the Knights of St John. See the clock tower and the (2) <u>nice</u> church of St Panteleimon.
* Don't miss the Archeological Musuem in the old Hospital of the Knights. It has got a (3) <u>nice</u> collection of objects from the different periods of Rhodes' history - Ancient Greek, Roman, Byzantine, and medieval.
* Go to the harbour - the original place of the Colossus of Rhodes, one of the seven wonders of the ancient world. The area near the harbour has got important buildings, for example the cathedral and the Town Hall.

Excursions
* Visit the town of Lindos, 47 kilometres from Rhodes. Walk around the medieval streets. Don't miss the (4) <u>nice</u> Acropolis with its (5) <u>nice</u> Temple of Athena.
Relax on the (6) <u>nice</u> Mediterranean beaches around the island.

Speaking: Speaking Game

> **'Where are you?'** Follow the stages below.

Stage 1
Imagine a holiday situation.

Example
Athens in Greece – sightseeing with a friend – walking around the Acropolis – looking at the shops – wearing a T-shirt and jeans

Stage 2
Work in pairs. Ask ten *Yes/No* questions. Find out where your partner is and what he/she is doing.

Example
A: (1) Are you at the beach?
B: No, I'm not.
A: (2) Are you in a city?
B: Yes, I am.

Talkback
Tell the class about your partner.

Example
George is in Athens. He is walking around the Acropolis.

10 Wildlife

In this module you...

- **Talk about** animals.
- **Read** and **listen to** dialogues.
- **Read and write** a description of an animal.
- **Learn about** *must/mustn't* and object pronouns.

Warm-up

pages 28–29

1 🔘 Listen and repeat.

KEY WORDS: Animals

chimp, golden eagle, kangaroo, koala, lion, llama, panda, penguin, tiger, wolf

What animals can you see in the photos?

Example A *panda*

2 Complete the table with two animals for each place. Some animals can go in more than one place.

Africa	
America (North and South)	
Asia	
Australia	
Europe	*golden eagle/wolf*

Add animals to the table. Use the Mini dictionary to help you.

3 Work in pairs. Ask and answer the questions.

1 What is your favourite animal?
2 What animal do you not like?
3 Have you got a pet at home? What is it?
4 Do you want a pet? What pet do you want?
5 Do you go to zoos or wildlife parks? Where do you go?

19 At the Wildlife Park

Before you start

A–Z

1 🔊 Listen and repeat.

KEY WORDS: Adjectives

dangerous, friendly, great, huge,
intelligent, interesting, lovely,
rare, strange

Look at the photo and the map
on page 69. Write five sentences
about the animals at the wildlife
park.

Example
*Elephants are huge animals but
they're not usually dangerous.*

Reading and Listening

2 🔊 Read and listen. Complete the dialogues with these words:

koalas, penguins, chimp, kangaroos, panda, dolphins

1
Teacher: OK. It's now ten o'clock. You must be back here at
twelve thirty.
Adam: Sorry? What time?
Teacher: Twelve thirty. Here at the coach. And you mustn't be late.
Kostas: What animals can we see? Are there (1) _____ ?
They're great.
Teacher: Yes, there are. Go and see the penguins and the
(2) _____ . And go and see the (3) _____ . It's lovely.
Paola: And our projects?
Teacher: Oh yes. You must choose two animals from one place.
For example, (4) _____ and (5) _____ . You must
complete the table in your file. And remember. You mustn't
copy the information!

2
Paola: Kostas. Take a photo of that (6) _____ . He's lovely!
Kostas: OK.
Adam: Do they like cheese sandwiches? Come here.
Gabriela: Don't Adam. You mustn't feed the animals.
Paola: And you mustn't give the animals our sandwiches!

must/mustn't
Presentation

3 Look at the examples with your teacher.

must	You **must** be back here at 12.30.
	You **must** choose two animals.
	You **must** complete the tables in your files.

mustn't	You **mustn't** be late.
	You **mustn't** copy!
	You **mustn't** feed the animals.
	You **mustn't** give the animals our sandwiches!

🔊 Listen and repeat.

Practice

4 Order the teacher's sentences about the animal project.

Example 1 *e*

a) Then, you must check your description.
b) Then, you must visit the animals, take photos and complete the table in your file.
c) You must use the tables to write a description of your animals.
d) Finally, you must use your description to write a poster. Add photos of the animals.
e) First, you must choose two animals.

5 Look at the signs. Write sentences about the Wildlife Park.

Example
You mustn't drop cans in the park.

6 Complete the school rules with *must* or *mustn't*.

1 You _____ wear your school uniform.
2 You _____ take pets to school.
3 You _____ be late for classes in the morning.
4 You _____ use mobile phones in class.
5 You _____ listen to your teachers in class.
6 You _____ talk in the school library.
7 You _____ eat in the library.
8 You _____ speak English in your English classes.

Now write five rules about your school.

Prepositions **near, next to**

7 Look at the map of the zoo and the prepositions in the sentences.

1 The llama is *next to* the kangaroos.
2 The lion is *not next to* the elephant.
3 The lion is *near* the elephant.
4 The chimps are *not near* the panda.

8 Work in pairs. Say true and false sentences with *next to* and *near*.

Example
A: *The camel is next to the chimps.*
B: *True!*

👉 Now do *Extra Time 19* on page 122.

20 Rare Animals

Before you start

1 Which of these animals are now very rare? Tell the class.

camels, European bison, imperial eagles, kangaroos, pandas, penguins, tigers

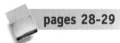 **pages 28-29**

2 🔘 Listen and repeat.

KEY WORDS: Parts of Animals

body, ears, eyes, head, legs, wings

Read this description. What animal is it?

It hasn't got wings. It's got small eyes. It's got a very big body. It's got huge ears. It's from Africa.

3 Work in pairs. Write a description of an animal.

Then read your description to another pair. They guess the animal.

Reading and Listening

4 🔘 Read and listen. Correct the mistakes in the dialogue.

Gabriela: Look at that animal. Look at it. It's got a huge (1) <u>head</u> and a big (2) <u>body</u>. What is it?

Adam: That's a bison. Bison are interesting animals.

Kostas: We haven't got them in Greece. Tell us about them.

Adam: Well, in Europe, they're very, very rare. They live in forests in Poland. In America there are thirty thousand American bison.

Gabriela: And what are those birds?

Paola: I don't know. Eagles, I think. Give me the brochure.

Kostas: Imperial Eagles. They're very, very rare. They live in Turkey, Greece and Spain.

Adam: Look at that eagle!

Kostas: Yes, she's lovely. Look at her.

Paola: How do you know it's a 'she', Kostas?

Kostas: Well, she's very big. She's got very big (3) <u>ears</u>. That eagle there is a male. Look at him. He's small.

Paola: Oh.

Kostas: And look at their (4) <u>legs</u>. Do you know? Imperial Eagles can see very well.

Paola: Yes, those eagles are looking at you, Adam. I think they're hungry!

Adam: Ha, ha!

Gabriela: I think they're lovely. Kostas, have you got your camera? Take a photo!

OBJECT PRONOUNS
Presentation

5 🔲 **Look at the examples with your teacher. Listen and repeat.**

Subject Pronouns	Object Pronouns
I don't know.	Give **me** the brochure.
Have **you** got your camera?	They're looking at **you**.
He's small.	Look at **him**.
She's got very big wings.	Look at **her**.
It's got big eyes.	Look at **it**.
We haven't got them in Greece.	Tell **us** about them.
They live in Greece.	Look at **them**!

Practice

6 **Complete the sentences with object pronouns.**

1 I don't know that word. Give _____ a dictionary, please.
2 My brother knows about animals. Ask _____ .
3 Where's my sister? Tell _____ the bus is ready to go.
4 Those birds are lovely. Look at _____ .
5 Our teacher gives _____ tests every week.
6 Look at _____ . Your clothes are black!

7 **Choose the correct word to complete the description.**

We've got two cats and a dog at home. (1) *My/Me* mum and dad love (2) *their/them*. My favourite is the dog – Cleopatra. I take (3) *her/she* out in the evenings. The cats sleep in (4) *my/me* bedroom and (5) *they/them* go out at night. Cleopatra doesn't like (6) *they/them*! In the garden, we've got a rabbit. The cats and Cleopatra want to eat (7) *it/its*, but it just looks at (8) *they/them*!

8 **Re-write the description. Replace the underlined words with pronouns and possessive adjectives.**

Example
Jack and I study French. Our teacher is very good.

Jack and I study French. <u>Jack's and my</u> teacher is very good. <u>The teacher</u> gives <u>Jack and me</u> homework every day. <u>Jack and I</u> like French but <u>French</u> is difficult. Jack likes reading easy books in French. The teacher gives <u>easy books in French</u> to <u>Jack</u>. <u>The teacher</u> is from France and <u>the teacher's</u> name is Marie Leblanc. <u>The teacher's</u> daughter is in <u>Jack's and my</u> class. <u>The teacher's daughter</u> is very good at French. <u>Jack and I</u> ask <u>the teacher's daughter</u> questions. <u>The teacher's daughter</u> helps <u>Jack and I</u> with <u>Jack's and my</u> homework.

🔲 **Listen and check your answers.**

Now do *Extra Time 20* on page 122.

Communication Workshop

Writing: A Description of an Animal

1 Read the description of the puma. Complete the table.

name?	*Puma (felis concolor)*
from?	
habitat? (where it lives)	
physical appearance?	
food?	
number of babies?	
common/rare?	

The Puma (felis concolor)

Gabriela Fernandez

Pumas (or cougars) are from North and South America. (1) <u>They</u> live in forests and mountains. They are big cats (1.80 m. long /90 kg). (2) <u>They</u> have got small heads and small ears. They are brown or yellow. They have got long legs and can jump 10 metres. Pumas live to 12 years old in the wild but (3) <u>they</u> live to 19 years old in zoos. Pumas eat big animals (e.g. sheep). They hunt (4) <u>them</u> in the day or night. Female pumas have one to five babies. (5) <u>They</u> live with their mother for two years. Now pumas are very rare in many areas of America (e.g. Florida in the United States).

2 Read the description again. What do the underlined pronouns refer to?

Example
1 *pumas*

Write a description of an animal. Follow the stages below.

Stage 1

Choose an animal. Find information about it. Copy and complete the table in Exercise 1.

Stage 2

Use your notes to write your description.

Stage 3

Check your description for spelling. Write your description neatly. Add a photo or drawing.

Speaking: Talk about the Animal

Find out about your partner's animal. Follow the stages below.

Stage 1

Match the questions with the headings in the table in Writing Exercise 1.

Example
name? What's their name?

What do they eat? Where are they from? How many babies do they have? Where do they live? Are they common? Are they big or small? What's their name?

Stage 2

Work in pairs. Ask and answer the questions about animals.

Talkback

Tell the class about your partner's animal.

Example
It's a bear. It lives in …

Review

Grammar

1 Look at the drawing of a wild animal park. Write eight more sentences using the Present Continuous (affirmative/negative).

Example
The teacher (1) is looking at the map.

2 Write questions about the people in the picture. Use these verbs.

(1) do, look at; (2) eat, sit, talk; (3) take; (4) take; (5) give; (6) drink

3 Complete the sentences with object pronouns.

1 Where are my books? Can you give _____ to _____ , please?
2 Look at _____. She's wearing a huge red hat!
3 Can you take a photo of _____ , please? Here's our camera.
4 Look at the story on page 98. Read _____ for your homework.
5 Who's that boy in the photo? Do you know _____?

4 Complete the sentences with *must/mustn't* about your English class.

1 You _____ speak English in class.
2 You _____ come to class late.
3 You _____ do your homework.
4 You _____ come to class with your Mini-dictionary.
5 You _____ check your writing.
6 You _____ speak French in class.

Vocabulary

5 Complete the mobile phone conversation with the correct verbs.

'Hi, I'm at the wildlife park. I'm
(1) ___eating___ a sandwich and
(2) _____ a cup of tea. A young boy is (3) _____ photos of a camel. There is a group of school children. The teacher is
(4) _____ a map. A boy is
(5) _____ a banana to the lion. Oh no! A chimp is (6) _____ one of my sandwiches!'

6 Complete the sentences with these prepositions.

in, at, near, next

1 I'm _____ London. I'm standing _____ Hyde Park.
2 The dolphins are _____ to the penguins.
3 My sister is _____ home now.
4 My dad is _____ the United States.
5 Pete is standing _____ me.
6 Are you _____ school?

Pronunciation: Word Stress

7 🔊 Listen to these words. Look at the main stress.

sightseeing ca**the**dral chimpan**zee**

Look at the words below. Mark the main stress.

kangaroo, excursion, athletics, collection, fantastic, animal, family, tomato, Egyptian, museum, beautiful, historic, piano, afternoon, computer, grandmother

🔊 Listen and check your answers. Listen again and repeat the words.

Culture Corner 5

BRITISH WILDLIFE

1 Read the captions and match them with the right pictures. Use the Mini-dictionary (pages 28–29) to help you.

A

1 Robins are common visitors to people's gardens in winter.

B

2 Golden eagles are now very rare. You can only see them in the mountains of Wales and Scotland.

3 There are two species of deer in Britain – red deer and fallow deer. Red deer are very big and live in Scotland.

4 Foxes are common and you can sometimes see them in gardens in Britain's big cities!

E

C

D

5 Red squirrels are now very rare in Britain. You can only find them in the Lake District, Scotland and some of the islands.

2 Write sentences about three animals from your country.

Learning Power!

Check your Language

1 Look at *Clothes* in the Mini-dictionary (page 25). Write down examples of clothes in your vocabulary book. Write example sentences about *you*.

Example
hat – I've got an old, black hat.

2 Look at other picture sections of the Mini-dictionary. Test your vocabulary. Cover up the words with pieces of paper. Look at the pictures and write down the words. Then check your answers.

3 Find the grammar boxes in this book.

Example a) *to be – Lessons 1, 2 and 3*

a) *to be* b) *have/has got* c) *can/can't*
d) *there is/are* e) Present Simple
f) Present Continuous g) *must/mustn't*

Write *your* example sentences.

Example *to be – I am from Athens.
My name is George.*

A

B

11 Memories

In this module you...

- **Talk about** memories and the past.
- **Read** and **listen to** dialogues.
- **Read** and **write** a description of your first school.
- **Learn about** the Past Simple of *to be*.

Warm-up

1 **Match the photos with the memories.**

1 first day of school
2 birthday party
3 summer holiday

 page 23

2 **Order the months of the year.**

KEY WORDS: Months

February, August, June, December, October, May, September, March, November, January, July, April

🔊 Listen and repeat. What is your favourite month of the year?

📖 A–Z

3 🔊 **Listen and repeat.**

KEY WORDS: Ordinal Numbers

first, second, third, fourth, fifth, sixth, seventh, eighth, ninth, tenth, eleventh, twelfth, thirteenth, fourteenth, fifteenth, sixteenth, seventeenth, eighteenth, nineteenth, twentieth, twenty-first, twenty-second, thirtieth, thirty-first

🔊 Listen and write down the dates.

Example
1 *the nineteenth of February*

4 **Look at this sentence.**

*My dad's birthday is **on** the tenth of June.*

Write down the dates of these birthdays.

your birthday, a friend's birthday, two family birthdays

C

21 Do You Remember?

Alton Towers

Shakespeare' House

Aldburgh Beach

Greetings

London Eye

Before you start

1 Look at the places in the photos. Do you think they are:

a) very interesting!
b) interesting
c) not very interesting
d) boring!

Can you think of similar places in your country?

A–Z

2 🔊 Listen and repeat.

KEY WORDS: Adjectives

asleep, cold, happy, late, nervous

Match these adjectives with their opposites in the Key Words:

hot, early, relaxed, sad, awake

Reading and Listening

3 🔊 Read and listen. Complete the dialogue with the adjectives in Exercise 2.

Kostas: Hey. Look at these postcards. Do you remember the trip to Stratford?

Gabriela: Yes, I do. It was very (1) _____ . And the teacher! She was very (2) _____ . We were (3) _____ for the bus.

Paola: *You* were late Gabi. I wasn't! I was early for the bus.

Adam: And we were in that restaurant next to the theatre. Do you remember? We weren't very (4) _____ .

Kostas: Yes, the food wasn't very good. It was (5) _____ .

Paola: But the play was great! *Hamlet* was fantastic.

Adam: Yes, it was great!

Kostas: What do you mean, Adam? You were (6) _____ for half of the play!

Adam: No, I wasn't.

was/were (1)
Presentation

4 Look at the examples with your teacher.

Affirmative	I	**was**	early.
	You/We/You/They	**were**	late.
	He/She	**was**	nervous.
	It	**was**	cold.
Negative	I	**was not (wasn't)**	late.
	You/We/You/They	**were not (weren't)**	very happy.
	He/She/It	**was not (wasn't)**	very good.

🎧 Listen and repeat.

Practice

5 Correct the sentences about the trip.

Example
1 *It wasn't very cold in Stratford. It was very hot there.*

1 It was very cold in Stratford.
2 The teacher was late for the bus.
3 The four students were very nervous.
4 The food was very good.
5 The food in the restaurant was hot.
6 The play, *Hamlet*, wasn't very good.
7 Gabriela was asleep in the play.

6 Use Megan's diary to write sentences.

Example
On the first of July she was in Cambridge with Gabriela and Paola. They were at King's College Chapel.

July

1 in Cambridge with Gabi and Paola – at King's College Chapel

2 at home with Mum – in the evening at Grandmother's house

3 at school with Jamie – Gabi and Paola in Stratford

4 school geography trip to Aldburgh – beach fantastic!

5 at school sports day – 2nd in the 100 metres!!!

6 very hot – at swimming pool with Gabriela, Paola, Adam and Kostas

7 with Gabi, Paola, Adam and Kostas at Alton Towers – great!

Prepositions **on, at, in**

7 Look at the prepositions of time.

1 **on** Monday morning
2 **at** six o'clock yesterday
3 **on** Saturday night
4 **at** eight o'clock this morning
5 **on** Sunday
6 **on** Friday afternoon
7 **in** August
8 **on** the tenth of May
9 **in** July
10 **at** two o'clock yesterday

Use the times to write sentences about your life. Include one or two false sentences.

Example
On Monday morning I was *at* school.

8 Work in pairs. Tell your partner where you were. Guess the false sentences.

Example
A: *In August, I was on holiday in France.*
B: *False.*
A: *No, true! I was with my family.*

👉 Now do *Extra Time 21* on page 123.

eye

eye

77

22 My First Memory

Before you start

page 24 and *A–Z*

1 Listen and repeat.

KEY WORDS: Weather
cold, hot, rainy, sunny, snowy

Look at the pictures of Adam and Gabriela's memories. What is the weather like?

Reading and Listening

2 Read and listen. Check your answers to Exercise 1.

Adam: What's your first memory, Gabi?
Gabriela: I think it was when I was four. I was with my sister and our dog, Pili.
Adam: Where were you?
Gabriela: I was at home in Rosario – in the garden.
Adam: What was the weather like?
Gabriela: It was very hot and it was sunny.
Adam: Were you happy?
Gabriela: Yes, I was. It was a fantastic day.

Adam: My first memory is very different. I was about three.
Gabriela: Who were you with?
Adam: My grandmother. We were at the shops in Kraków.
Gabriela: And what was the weather like? Was it cold?
Adam: Yes, it was. And it was snowy.
Gabriela: Were you cold?
Adam: No, I wasn't. I was very happy! It was Christmas!

was/were (2): QUESTIONS
Presentation

3 Look at the examples with your teacher.

'Yes/No' Questions + Short Answers	Were you happy? Was it cold?	Yes, I **was**. No, I **wasn't**. Yes, it **was**. No, it **wasn't**.
Wh- Questions	Who **were** you with? What **was** the weather like? Where **were** you?	

[○○] Listen and repeat.

Practice

4 Order the words to write questions.

Example
1 *How old were you?*

1 you/were/how old
2 with/were/you/who
3 you/where/were
4 like/was/what/the weather
5 happy/you/were

Answer the questions for Gabriela and Adam.

Example
1 *I was four. (Gabriela)*

5 Write questions for these answers.

Example
1 *Where were you?*

1 At my grandfather's house.
2 It was cold and rainy.
3 No, I wasn't cold.
4 With my dad and my grandpa.
5 It was three o'clock in the afternoon.
6 Yes, I was. Very happy!

page 22

6 Find these times in the Key Words.

9.45, 9.05, 9.15, 9.50, 9.30, 9.35, 9.25

KEY WORDS: Times

nine o'clock, five past nine, ten past nine, quarter past nine, twenty past nine, twenty-five past nine, half past nine, twenty-five to ten, twenty to ten, quarter to ten, ten to ten, five to ten, ten o'clock

[○○] Listen and repeat.

7 Write sentences about where you were yesterday at these times.

Example
At quarter to nine I was on the school bus.

8.45a.m., 11.15a.m., 1.30p.m., 3.20p.m., 4.40p.m., 5.05p.m., 6.25p.m., 7.50p.m., 9.00p.m., 11.30p.m.

Work in pairs. Ask and answer questions.

Example
A: *Where were you at quarter to nine in the morning?*
B: *I was on the school bus – with you!*

8 Use the cues to write sentences about your first memory.

Example
I was at home. I was with my ...

1 where?
2 how old?
3 who with?
4 what time?
5 happy?
6 weather?

9 Work in pairs. Ask and answer questions about your first memory.

☞ Now do *Extra Time 22* on page 123.

Communication Workshop

I remember my first school very well. It was not very big <u>but</u> it was a very good school. The school was near to the centre of town. I can remember my first classroom now. It was a very big room with four small windows. The walls were white with posters and pictures on them.

I was very young <u>and</u> I was very nervous the first day. Some classes were difficult <u>but</u> I was very happy at the school. My first teacher was fantastic. His name was Mr John Papadaki. He was a very good teacher. My favourite activity was reading. My two best friends at the school were George and Petros. Petros is in my class now. He is sitting next to me!

Writing: A Description of Your First School

1 Read Kostas's description. Order the topics he mentions.

Example 1 *the school*

my best friends, the classroom, my first day, my teacher, the school

2 Look at the examples of *but* and *and* in the text. Use the words to write sentences with *but* or *and*.

1 school: small + good   3 teacher: young + friendly
2 classroom: new + cold   4 classes: difficult + interesting

Write a description of your first school. Follow the stages below.

Stage 1
Write notes about these things.

location of school – classroom – teachers – favourite activities – best friends at school

Stage 2
Use your notes to write about your school. Check for:

spelling ✓ punctuation ✓
correct use of *was/were* ✓

Speaking: Telling Memories

Talk about your first school. Follow the stages below.

Stage 1
Write five questions to ask your partner about his/her first school memories.

Example
Where was your first school? Who was your teacher?

Stage 2
Work in pairs. Ask and answer questions about your schools.

Example
A: *Where was your first school?*
B: *It was near my house.*

Talkback
Tell the class one or two interesting things about your partner's memories.

Example
Pablo's teacher was my aunt!

12 At night

In this module you...

- Talk about the past and about television.
- Read and listen to dialogues.
- Read and write an e-mail message.
- Read a TV page.
- Learn about *there was/there were* and past time expressions.

Warm-up

1 Look at the photo. Who do you think are 'morning people' and who are not?

2 Work in pairs. Do the questionnaire. Is your partner a day or night person?

Are You a Day or Night Person?

1 When do you feel tired?
a) in the morning b) in the afternoon
c) at night

2 At the weekend, do you go to bed ...
a) before 10 o'clock? b) before midnight?
c) after midnight?

3 Do you do your homework
a) before school? b) when you get back home?
c) before you go to bed?

4 When do you like doing exercise?
a) before school b) in the morning
c) in the evening

pages 14–15

3 🔲 Check the meaning of the Key Words. Listen and repeat.

> **KEY WORDS: Meals**
> breakfast, lunch, tea, dinner

What times are meals in your country?
Example
We have lunch at one o'clock.

Prepositions before, after

4 Look at the examples of *before* and *after*.

On school days, **before** breakfast I get up and have a shower. At the weekend, **before** breakfast I watch TV. On school days, **after** lunch I play basketball.

Write sentences about what you do on school days and at the weekend:

before breakfast, after lunch, before dinner, after dinner, before you go to bed.

23 Out and About

Before you start

A–Z

1 Look at the Key Words. What places can you see in the photos?

KEY WORDS: Places

amusement arcade, bowling alley, cinema, coffee bar, concert, fast-food restaurant, Internet café, library, takeaway

Listen and repeat.

Reading and Listening

2 Read and listen. Complete the dialogue with Key Words.

Gabriela: Where were you last night, Adam? You weren't at home.

Adam: No, I was in town with some friends. We were in the (1) _____ yesterday evening. It was great.

Gabriela: Oh, yes. I was there last week with Megan. It's brilliant.

Adam: And we were at that new (2) _____ , near the (3) _____ .

Gabriela: Oh, yes? Who were you with? Were you with that French girl yesterday?

Adam: No, I wasn't! I was with some friends. We were in the same class last year. And guess who was there.

Gabriela: I can't guess. The Queen?

Adam: Don't be silly. No, Kostas and Megan.

Gabriela: Really? She wasn't at home yesterday afternoon or evening. She was 'in the (4) _____ '! And she was with Kostas in the (5) _____ yesterday morning.

Adam: This is getting interesting!

TIME EXPRESSIONS WITH *was* AND *were*
Presentation

3 Look at the examples with your teacher.

Yesterday	Last
We were in the amusement arcade **yesterday evening.**	Where were you **last night**?
Were you with that French girl **yesterday**?	I was there **last week** …
She wasn't at home **yesterday afternoon.**	We were in the same class **last year.**
She was with Kostas **yesterday morning.**	

🔊 Listen and repeat.

Practice

4 Correct these sentences about the characters.

Example
1 *Adam wasn't in the amusement arcade yesterday afternoon. He was there yesterday evening.*

1 Adam was in the amusement arcade yesterday afternoon.
2 He was with a French girl last night.
3 Gabriela was in the amusement arcade last month.
4 Adam and his friends were in the same class last week.
5 Megan was in the library yesterday morning.
6 Kostas was at home yesterday morning.
7 Kostas and Megan were in the coffee bar yesterday evening.

5 Use these words to write questions.

1 were/you/night?/where/last
2 who/yesterday/you/with/afternoon?/were
3 you/were/yesterday?/in the library
4 year?/in London/last/he/was
5 with your friends/last/were/you/week?

6 Where were you and who were you with:

last night/week/year?
yesterday morning/afternoon?

Write sentences and include two false pieces of information.

7 Work in pairs. Ask and answer questions. Guess the false information.

Example
A: *Where were you last night?*
B: *I was at the cinema with Britney Spears.*
A: *False!*
B: *That's right. I was at home.*

☞ Now do *Extra Time 23* on page 123.

24 Staying In

Television

Channel 1

5.00	**The Simpsons.** Homer has problems!
5.35	**Neighbours.** Australian soap.
6.00	**News and weather.**
7.00	**Tiger, Tiger.** The problems of the rare Bengal tiger – what can we do?
8.15	**Win A Million!** Two teams play games to win big money prizes.
10.00	**News and weather.**
10.45	**Classic Cinema:** *On The River.* Western with Clint Eastwood.

102

Before you start

A–Z

1 🔊 Check the meaning of the Key Words. Listen and repeat.

KEY WORDS: TV Programmes

cartoon, comedy, documentary, film, game show, news, soap, sports programme

What kind of programmes are in the photos?

Reading and Listening

2 Read the TV guide. Classify the programmes.

Example
The Simpsons – cartoon

3 What is your favourite programme? Tell the class.

4 🔊 Read and listen. What were the characters' opinions of these things?

a) the documentary on tigers,
b) *Neighbours,*
c) the Clint Eastwood film,
d) the tennis,
e) the jazz concert

Example
a) Paola – not very good

Kostas: Were there any good programmes on TV last night? I was out.
Paola: No, there weren't. There was a documentary about tigers, but it wasn't very good. And there weren't any good soaps. *Neighbours* was terrible!
Kostas: Was there a good film on?
Paola: No, there wasn't.
Adam: Yes, there was! There was a western with Clint Eastwood in it. It was great. There wasn't a football match. But there was a good tennis match from the Australian Open.
Paola: So where were you last night, Kostas?
Kostas: I was in town with a friend.
Adam: You mean Megan?
Kostas: Yes, that's right. After our tennis class we were at a jazz concert with her dad. There were people from her school at the concert. It was great!

Television

Channel 2

4.30	**Tour de France.** In the Alps.
5.30	**Tennis.** Australian Open.
7.15	**Friends.** Monica arrives late!
8.00	**Life On Earth.** Repeat of the classic wildlife series.
9.00	**Film Night.** *Alien 1v.* Science fiction thriller, starring Sigourney Weaver.
10.45	**Newsnight.** Today's news and interviews with Jeremy Paxman.

103

There was/There were
Presentation

5 Look at the examples with your teacher.

	Singular	Plural
Affirmative	**There was** a documentary about tigers.	**There were** people from her school.
Negative	**There wasn't** a football match.	**There weren't** any good soaps.
Questions	**Was there** a good film on?	**Were there** any good programmes on TV last night?
Short Answers	Yes, **there was.** No, **there wasn't.**	Yes, **there were.** No, **there weren't.**

Listen and repeat.

Practice

6 Use the cues to write sentences about the programmes.

Example
1 There was a documentary about tigers.

1 documentary about tigers (✓)
2 a football match (✗)
3 two films (✓)
4 a game show (✓)
5 any good soaps (✗)
6 a comedy film (✗)

Use the cues to write questions and short answers.

Example
1 A: *Was there a documentary about tigers?*
    B: *Yes, there was.*

7 Look at the TV guide again. Choose programmes you think are probably:

very interesting, OK, boring, funny, exciting

Example
Friends – funny
documentary on tigers – interesting

8 Work in pairs. Take turns. Student A was out last night. Student B tells him/her about programmes on TV last night.

Example
A: *Were there any good sports programmes on TV last night?*
B: *Yes, there was a good tennis game.*

9 Work in pairs. Talk about the programmes on TV in your country.

Example
A: *There was a football match on last night.*
B: *Yes, there was. It was boring! There was a good film, Life Is Beautiful.*
A: *Yes, it was brilliant.*

☞ Now do *Extra Time 24* on page 123.

85

Communication Workshop

Writing: A Personal e-mail

1 Check the meaning of the Key Words.

KEY WORDS: Adjectives

angry, bored, funny, happy, nervous, sad, surprised, worried

2 Use the key below to re-write the message in full sentences.

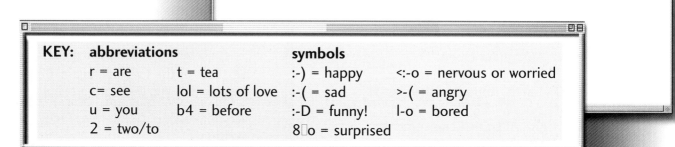

Hi Jamie,

How r u? I'm very :-) . It's the weekend. B4 t, there was a good programme on TV. It was very :-D!
Tom is very :-(. His exam yesterday was terrible. Now he is <:-o about the results. Dad is very >-(!
My exams were OK. Now I am l-o.
R u OK? Tom says hello 2 u! C u soon.
Lol
Carol xxx

KEY:

abbreviations		symbols	
r = are	t = tea	:-) = happy	<:-o = nervous or worried
c= see	lol = lots of love	:-(= sad	>-(= angry
u = you	b4 = before	:-D = funny!	l-o = bored
2 = two/to		8▢o = surprised	

Write an e-mail message to a friend. Follow the stages.

Stage 1
Think of a situation for you and your family or friends, e.g. at the weekend, in the evening, on holiday.

Stage 2
Look at the symbols in the key. Decide on your, your friends', and your family's feelings.

Example
sister l-o *(her friends are on holiday)*

Stage 3
Use the symbols and abbreviations to write a similar message to Carol's. Include information about you and your family.

Talkback
Give your message to your partner. He/She writes it in full sentences.

Speaking: A Night Out

Talk about a very good or very bad night out. Follow the stages.

Stage 1
Write notes about your night out.

- when: *last month/in August/last year*
- weather: *cold/rainy/warm*
- who with: *your friends/your sister/your uncle*
- where: *a concert/a party/a disco*

Stage 2
Work in pairs. Ask and answer questions.

Example
A: *When was your night out?*
B: *It was last year. I was on holiday.*
A: *Who were you with?*

Talkback
Tell the class things about your partner's holiday.

Example
She was on holiday with Carolina. The weather was warm. There was a good disco near her hotel.

Review

Grammar

1 Complete the dialogue with the correct form of *was* or *were*.

A: What is the best holiday memory you have?
B: I (1) _____ ten and we (2) _____ in the Channel Islands, in Guernsey.
A: What time of year (3) _____ you there?
B: It (4) _____ (not) August. I think it (5) _____ June or July. It (6) _____ hot and sunny and there (7) _____ a fantastic beach. Our hotel (8) _____ near the beach and there (9) _____ small bars and cafés next to it. There (10) _____ fantastic ice-creams!
A: Who (11) _____ you with?
B: I (12) _____ with my mum and dad, my sister and my granny. We (13) _____ there for two weeks. And there (14) _____ excursions – one to France and one to the little island of Sark.
A: Was the food good?
B: Yes, but I can remember one meal in a restaurant in St Peter's Port, the capital of Guernsey. I (15) _____ (not) very happy. The food (16) _____ (not) very good!

2 Write questions about the holiday.

Example
Where were you on holiday? We were in Guernsey.

1 _____ ? We were there in June or July.
2 _____ ? I was ten years old.
3 _____ ? I was with my family.
4 _____ ? Our hotel was near the beach.
5 _____ ? The weather was fantastic!

3 Complete the sentences with *last* or *yesterday*.

1 _____ night there was a good film on TV.
2 _____ week I was in London with my family.
3 I was at home _____ afternoon.
4 _____ year my granny was in hospital.
5 I was at school _____ morning.
6 There was a party at my school _____ month.
7 _____ afternoon there was a good game of tennis.
8 I was very tired _____ night.

Vocabulary

4 What was the weather like in your area last year? Complete the sentences.

1 It was sunny in _____ .
2 It was cold in _____ .
3 It was rainy in _____ .
4 It was snowy in _____ .
5 It was hot in _____ .

5 Write the dates.

Example
25/03   the twenty-fifth of March

1 14/01 _____   4 09/08 _____
2 15/05 _____   5 31/04 _____
3 03/11 _____

6 Complete the sentences with these adjectives:

tired, hot, bored, awake, happy, late, angry

1 At 3 o'clock this morning I wasn't awake. I was _____ .
2 It's very _____ in here. Open the window, please.
3 I feel very _____ . I want to go to bed and sleep for hours.
4 I was twenty minutes _____ for class. My teacher was very _____ .
5 This programme is terrible. I am _____ !
6 On Monday mornings I don't feel very _____ .

Pronunciation

7 🔊 Listen to the two sounds in October.
   a   b
   /ɒ/ /əʊ/
   O c t o b e r

🔊 Listen and classify the sounds (a or b) in these words.

go, got, old, not, on, cold, hot, snow, stop, know, soap, shop, drop, clock, boat

🔊 Listen again and repeat.

Culture Corner 6

Television in Britain

1 In British television there are five main channels. Two channels are public (BBC 1 and BBC 2) and three are private (ITV, Channel 4 and Channel 5).

2 The first daily TV programmes in the world were on the BBC in 1936.

3 There are also satellite channels, e.g. 'Sky'. You pay to watch these channels.

4 Famous British 'soaps' are *EastEnders* (about people in the east of London), *Coronation Street* (about a street in Manchester) and *Brookside* (about people in Liverpool). The first *Coronation Street* programme was in 1960!

5 BBC 1 and ITV often have popular quizzes and game shows.

6 BBC 2 and Channel 4 often have interesting educational programmes and documentaries.

7 On average, people in Britain watch 23 hours of TV per week!

1 Read about British television. Match the topics (a–g) with the paragraphs (1–7). Use the Mini-dictionary to help you.

a) satellite TV, b) history, c) soaps, d) educational programmes, e) channels, f) watching TV, g) popular programmes.

2 Write five sentences about television in your country.

Learning Power!

Do you remember?

1 Look at modules 1–11. Answer these questions:

1 Which modules were very interesting for you?
2 Which character in modules 1–11 was your favourite?
3 Which grammar items were difficult? (Look at the grammar boxes.) Which areas do you need to study?
4 Look at the Mini-dictionary. What vocabulary areas do you need to study?

2 How many words can you remember about:

1 places? 2 feelings? 3 television? 4 meals?

Now look at this module and add to your vocabulary list.

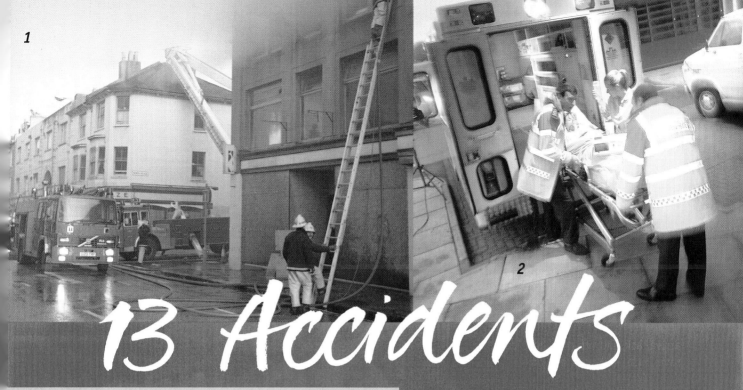

1

2

13 Accidents

In this module you ...

- Talk about the past.
- Read a leaflet.
- Read and listen to a photo story.
- Read and write a story.
- Learn about the Past Simple.

Warm-up

A–Z

1 What Key Words are similar in your language?

> **KEY WORDS**
> ambulance, fire brigade, hospital, police

pages 4–5

2 Find these people in the photos. Match their jobs with the Key Words above.

> **KEY WORDS: Jobs**
> ambulance driver, fire fighter, nurse, police officer

oo Listen and repeat.

Example
1 *fire fighter* ...

3 Work in pairs. Look at the photos. How are these things different or similar in your country? Tell the class.

1 the colour of uniforms of police officers, fire fighters and nurses
2 the colour of ambulances, police cars and fire engines

Example
In our country, police officers don't wear blue uniforms, they wear green uniforms.

3

25 Watch Out!

Before you start

A–Z

1 🔊 Listen and repeat. Check the meaning of the Key Words. Then match them with the words below.

KEY WORDS: Verbs

arrive, ask, fall off, give, hit, leave, save, turn, wake up, put on

clothes, your bicycle, at school, a question, a corner, your house, a person, in the morning, a present

Example
arrive at school

Reading and Listening

2 🔊 Put the story in the right order. Listen and check your answers.

PAST SIMPLE AFFIRMATIVE: REGULAR VERBS
Presentation

3 Look at the examples with your teacher.

Regular Verbs

A van **turn<u>ed</u>** a corner very fast.
The driver **stopp<u>ed</u>**.
The driver **phon<u>ed</u>** for an ambulance.
The police **arrived**.
A doctor **ask<u>ed</u>** some questions.
Your helmet **sav<u>ed</u>** you.

🔊 Listen and repeat.

A

Look out!

They **saw** a big car near a corner. A van **turned** the corner very fast and Adam **fell off** his bicycle! The driver **stopped**.

B

On Friday morning, Adam and Kostas **got up** and **had** breakfast. Then they **put on** their helmets and **went** to school by bicycle. They **left** their house at half-past eight.

C

You were lucky! Your helmet saved you.

Adam **woke up** in the hospital. At the hospital a doctor **asked** some questions and the nurses **gave** him some medicine.

Practice

4 Complete the sentences with these verbs.

arrive, ask, cook, phone, play, rain, stay, watch

1 I _____ computer games yesterday.
2 You _____ a difficult question!
3 He _____ at school at half-past nine this morning.
4 She _____ me at 8 o'clock.
5 It _____ last night.
6 We _____ in a nice hotel last August.
7 You _____ a lovely meal last night.
8 They _____ TV last night.

PAST SIMPLE AFFIRMATIVE: IRREGULAR VERBS

Presentation

5 Look at the examples with your teacher.

> **Irregular Verbs**
>
> Adam and Kostas **had** breakfast.
> They **left** their house at half-past eight.
> They **went** to school by bicycle.
> They **put on** their helmets.
> They **saw** a big car near a corner.
> Adam **fell off** his bicycle.
> The ambulance **took** Adam to the hospital.
> Adam **woke up** in the hospital.
> The nurses **gave** him some medicine.

🔊 Listen and repeat.

*Adam **was** unconscious! The driver **phoned** for an ambulance and the police. The police **arrived** and then the ambulance **took** Adam to the hospital.*

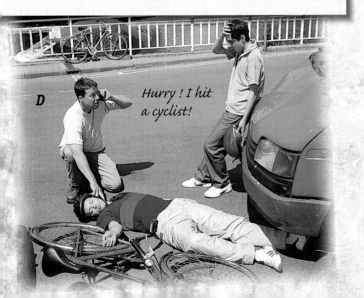

D

Hurry ! I hit a cyclist!

6 Match the past forms in Exercise 5 with their infinitives.

go, see, put on, have, fall off, leave, take, give, wake up

Practice

7 Complete the sentences with the verbs in the Past Simple form.

Adam: I (1) _____ (leave) the house at half-past eight with Kostas. We (2) _____ (go) to school on our bikes. We (3) _____ (see) a car near a corner and a van (4) _____ (turn) the corner. I (5) _____ (fall off) my bike.
Kostas: Yes, I (6) _____ (stay) with Adam and the driver (7) _____ (phone) for help. The police (8) _____ (arrive) in five minutes and then an ambulance (9) _____ (take) him to the hospital.
Adam: I (10) _____ (wake up) in the hospital!

8 Write six sentences about what you did yesterday. Include one false sentence. Use these verbs in the Past Simple form.

go, have, leave, phone, wake up, watch

Example
I went to the cinema with Lydia.

Work in pairs. Tell your partner about yesterday. He/She guesses the false sentence.

Example
A: *I went to the bowling alley with my dad.*
B: *True.*
A: *No, false!*

9 Read the story again and look at the pictures. Then close your books. Work in pairs and re-tell the story.

Example
A: *On Friday morning, Adam and Kostas had breakfast and they left the house at half-past seven.*
B: *No, it was half-past eight, I think.*

👉 Now do *Extra Time 25* on page 123.

26 Road Safety

1 Match the Key Words with the numbers in the photos.

KEY WORDS

cyclist, driver, helmet, junction, motorcyclist, pedestrian, seat belt, zebra crossing

🔊 Listen and repeat.

Reading

2 Read the text. Are these sentences true (T) or false (F)?

1 The first death in a car crash was in 1899. ☐

2 Nine hundred motorcyclists died on the road in 1998. ☐

3 The law changed in 1979 and then motorcyclists had to wear helmets. ☐

4 Accidents with cyclists are common in the 15–17 age group. ☐

5 Accidents with pedestrians usually happen on or near zebra crossings. ☐

3 Why do you think there are accidents on or near zebra crossings?

ROAD SAFETY
IN BRITAIN

FACTFILE

The first death in a car accident in Britain was on 23 February, 1899. A driver turned a corner at a speed of 40 kph and the car crashed. In those days, cars didn't have seat belts and the driver died. In 1998, a survey showed the following information:

Road Users Deaths
Drivers 1,850
Motorcyclists 500
Cyclists 150
Pedestrians 900

For many years motorcyclists took risks because they didn't wear helmets and many motorcyclists died. The law changed in 1972. Then motorcyclists had to wear helmets to protect their heads.

The survey showed that the majority of bicycle accidents were with boys 12–15 years old. The survey showed that these boys had accidents because:
– they didn't look before they turned right,
– they didn't stop at a junction,
– cars didn't see them.

The survey also showed that 20% of accidents with pedestrians happened on or near a zebra crossing. It didn't show why.

PAST SIMPLE: AFFIRMATIVE AND NEGATIVE

Presentation

4 Look at the examples with your teacher.

	Affirmative	Negative
Regular Verbs	The van driver **stopped**.	They **didn't (did not) stop** at a junction.
	A survey **showed** that …	The survey **didn't (did not) show** why …
Irregular Verbs	They **had** accidents because …	Cars **didn't (did not) have** seat belts.
	Adam and Kostas **saw** a van.	Cars **didn't (did not) see** them.

Listen and repeat.

5 Read the Factfile again. <u>Underline</u> more examples of Past Simple forms, affirmative or negative. Write the infinitives.

Practice

6 Correct these sentences – the underlined words are wrong.

Example
1 *I didn't see the cyclist.*

1 *I didn't <u>saw</u> the cyclist.*
2 *You didn't <u>looked</u> before you turned.*
3 *He didn't <u>stopped</u> at the junction.*
4 *She didn't <u>took</u> any risks.*
5 *It didn't <u>happened</u> near a zebra crossing.*
6 *We didn't <u>went</u> by car.*
7 *You didn't <u>wore</u> your helmet!*
8 *They didn't <u>had</u> seat belts.*

7 Complete the sentences with the verbs in the Past Simple form.

1 I _____ (go) to bed early and _____ (not see) the match.
2 You _____ (not phone) me before you _____ (leave) the station.
3 He _____ (knock) down a pedestrian but he _____ (not stop)!
4 She _____ (not go) to his party but she _____ (give) him a present.
5 We _____ (wake) up late and _____ (not have) time for breakfast.
6 They _____ (take) their helmets but they _____ (not wear) them!

8 Work in pairs. Guess five things your partner did yesterday.

Example
A: *You watched the match on TV.*
B: *No, I didn't watch the match on TV. You did your maths homework.*
A: *Yes, I did my maths homework.*

Prepositions **at, for, off, to, up**

9 Complete the sentences with these words.

at, for, off, to, up

1 She woke _____ at 8 o'clock.
2 He fell _____ his motorbike.
3 They arrived _____ school late.
4 We phoned _____ a taxi.
5 A bus took us _____ the hotel.

☞ Now do *Extra Time 26* on page 124.

Communication Workshop

Writing: A Story

1 Read the story of an accident.

I was in Oxford last month on an English course. I was in a house with a Brazilian boy, Manuel. He had an accident on his bicycle. On Friday morning, we woke up, had breakfast <u>and then</u> left the house on our bicycles. We turned a corner, saw a cat <u>and then</u> Manuel crashed into the wall!

2 Look at '*and then*' in the story. Write sentences with '*and then*' and the words below.

Example
On Monday, I got up late, had a shower and then had a small breakfast.

1 (Monday) get up late/have shower/have breakfast
2 leave home/wait for bus/see a friend
3 arrive at school/have cup of coffee/go to class late
4 teacher be angry/ask me questions/give me extra homework

Write a story about an accident. Follow the stages.

Stage 1
Look at these verbs.

arrive, ask, crash, fall off, have, give, go, leave, look, phone, save, see, stop, take, wake up, wear

Use verbs from the list to plan your story. Put them on a timeline.

Example

go to friend's party	arrive at party	give her a present	see car in street
------X-----------	-----X-------------	----X----------	--X-----
8.30	9.00		10.00

Stage 2
Use your timeline to write your story in the past. Add details to make it interesting and include *and then*.

Example
Last Saturday I went to Anna's house. It was her birthday. I left my house at half-past eight. I arrived at the party, gave Anna a present and then ...

Stage 3
Check the verbs in your story (regular/irregular, affirmative/negative).

Speaking: Telling a Story

Tell your story. Follow the stages.

Stage 1
Practise reading your story.

Stage 2
Work in groups. Tell your story to the group.

Talkback
Vote for the best story in your group. Read it to the class.

14 Missing home

In this module you...

Warm-up

A–Z

1 Match the photos and the Key Words.

KEY WORDS

family, food, friends, pet,
TV programme, the weather

2 Work in pairs. Copy the table. You have three minutes to add words! Use the Mini-dictionary to help you.

Family	brother
Food	spaghetti
Pets	
TV programmes	
Weather	

3 Work in groups with another pair. Take turns to say words from your table. Who is the winner?

4 When you are away from home, what do you miss from your home?

- your pet?
- your friends?
- the food?
- the weather?
- your family?
- TV programmes?

5 Work in pairs. Ask and answer questions.

Example
A: *Do you miss your pet?*
B: *Yes, I miss my cat. And you?*
A: *I haven't got a pet. Do you miss ...*

27 Homesick

Before you start

 A–Z

1 🔊 **Listen and repeat. Match opposites in the Key Words box.**

> **KEY WORDS: Adjectives**
>
> bad, big, cold, early, easy, friendly, good, hard, hot, late, small, unfriendly

Example
bad/good

Reading and Listening

2 🔊 **What do Gabriela, Paola and Kostas miss? Read and listen to the dialogue.**

Gabriela, Paola and Kostas meet on Monday morning.

Gabriela: Well, we go home on Saturday.

Paola: Yes. Do you miss Argentina?

Gabriela: I miss some things. I miss my friends and my family, of course, and I miss my dogs!

Kostas: And I suppose you miss your sleep – you get up earlier here!

Gabriela: Very funny. The course was easier last year, Paola, but the people are friendlier this year. Do you miss Siena?

Paola: I miss some things. I miss my cat. And my mother's cooking is better than English food! But I don't miss Italian television – it's worse than English TV. What about you, Kostas?

Kostas: Well, I miss my computer – it's bigger and better than the computer I use here. And I miss the beach. But I like Cambridge – I love the art galleries.

Paola: Is it older than Rhodes?

Kostas: I don't know about that – but it's colder! Ah, here's Adam!

What do you think Adam misses or doesn't miss about Poland?

Practice

5 Write sentences.

Example
1 *Spain is hotter than Britain.*

1 Spain/hot/Britain
2 Italian food/good/English food
3 Poland/big/Britain
4 English weather/bad/Italian weather
5 Today/sunny/yesterday
6 Cambridge/small/London
7 London/noisy/Cambridge
8 Jamie/old/Megan

6 Write sentences about these things. Use the Key Words.

pop and film stars, food, TV programmes, countries, cities, school subjects, football players and teams

Example
Ricky Martin is better than Enrique Iglesias.

7 Work in pairs. Take turns to say your sentences.

Example
A: *I think history is easier than mathematics.*
B: *Yes, it is. I think …*

Prepositions in, at

8 Look at the examples. Then complete the sentences with *in* or *at*.

Examples
*I go to bed **at** 11 o'clock during the week, but later **at** the weekend.*
*They go on holiday **in** summer. They went to France **in** August.*

1 They go skiing _____ winter.
2 School starts _____ 9 o'clock.
3 My birthday is _____ March.
4 I saw a good film _____ the weekend.

☞ Now do *Extra Time 27* on page 124.

Comparatives (1)
Presentation

3 Look at the examples with your teacher.

Adjective	Comparative Form
old	old**er** (than)
big	big**ger** (than)
early	earl**ier** (than)
good	better (than)
bad	worse (than)

🔊 Listen and repeat the examples.

4 Make comparatives of the following adjectives:

cold, easy, funny, hot, noisy, small, sunny

28 Across the Atlantic

Before you start

page 24

1 Check the meaning of the Key Words. Match the Key Words with the photos.

KEY WORDS: SEASONS

autumn, spring, summer, winter

[∘∘] Listen and repeat.

2 When are the seasons in your country?

Example
Winter is in December, January and February.

Reading and Listening

3 Look at the people in the photos. What do you think Sarah misses about Britain? What does Brad miss about the USA?

the weather, TV programmes, sport, the food

Example
I think Sarah misses British TV programmes.

[∘∘] Read and listen to the text and check your guesses.

Sarah Halliwell is from Chester in the north of England but works with computers in California. What does she miss about Britain?

'I miss the green English countryside, especially in autumn and spring. It's more colourful than here – California is sunny all the time! I also miss the soaps on TV, like *Coronation Street* and *EastEnders* because they are more serious and more realistic than the soaps here. But I'm not homesick. I think the lifestyle and the food is healthier here.'

"I'm not homesick"

53

Brad Shaw

is from New York City but came to live in Doncaster in England five years ago. Does he miss New York?

'Well, I miss American sports. English cricket is boring, more boring than baseball. And I miss going out because the theatres, cafés and shops in New York are more interesting than here. But New York is noisier and more expensive than here, of course. I don't miss American television – I think English TV is better. And I don't miss the weather in New York – those very cold winters and very hot summers!'

"I miss American sports"

54

COMPARATIVES (2)
Presentation

4 Look at the examples with your teacher.

Adjective	Comparative Form
colourful	more colourful (than)
expensive	more expensive (than)
serious	more serious (than)

Listen and repeat.

Practice

5 Write sentences.

Example
Cricket is more boring than baseball.

1 Cricket/boring/baseball
2 His shirt/colourful/your shirt
3 Classical music/serious/pop music
4 Her drawing/interesting/my drawing
5 CDs/expensive/cassettes

6 Complete the sentences with the adjectives in the correct form.

My country is (1) _____ (big) than Britain and the weather is (2) _____ (sunny) here. I went to Britain last summer to learn English. English is (3) _____ (easy) than French. The countryside is (4) _____ (colourful) than here, but things are (5) _____ (expensive).

Write similar sentences. Compare *your* country with Britain.

7 Write three things you *like* about your country and three things you *don't like*.

Example
I like the beach in summer. I don't like the traffic.

Now work in pairs. Take turns to tell your partner what you *like* and *don't like* about your country.

Example
A: *I like the beach in summer.*
B: *Why?*
A: *Because I like swimming and the sunny weather.*

☞ Now do *Extra Time 28* on page 124.

99

Communication Workshop

Speaking: A Discussion

Compare big cities and small towns. Follow the stages.

Stage 1
Work in two groups.

Group A
Make a list of the good things about big cities and the bad things about small towns.

Example
good – cinemas; bad – no discos

Group B
Make a list of the good things about small towns and the bad things about big cities.

Example
good – cleaner than cities; bad – noise

Stage 2
Work in pairs, one student from Group A, one from Group B. Discuss life in cities and towns.

Example
A: *I think small towns are friendlier than big cities.*
B: *Yes, but there are no cinemas. And cities are more interesting at night.*

Talkback
Have a class vote. Are big cities better than small towns?

Writing: A Postcard

Before you start

1 Read the postcard. Who and what does Sergio miss about Britain?

Dear Steven,
I'm very tired (1) _____ I got back on Saturday (2) _____ school started today. Thanks for a great holiday. I miss you (3) _____ your friends – and I miss the sports club (4) _____ discos.
Can you send me Sandra's address (5) _____ I want to write her a letter. The weather here is hot (6) _____ sunny – I don't miss your English rain!
Write soon!
Sergio

Steven Banks,
14, Tower Street,
Coventry,
UK.

2 Complete the gaps in the postcard with *and* or *because*.

Imagine you visited a penfriend in Britain. Write a postcard to him/her. Follow the stages.

Stage 1
Make a list of what you *miss/don't miss* about Britain. Think about these things:

food, places, people, shops, TV programmes, weather

Stage 2
Draw a postcard (15cm x 10cm). Invent the address of your friend and write the postcard.

Talkback
In pairs, read your postcards. Who misses Britain more?

Review

Grammar

1 Write the verbs in the Past Simple.

1 Adam _____ (fall) and _____ (hit) his head on the ground. He _____ (be) unconscious for fifteen minutes but _____ (feel) better when he _____ (wake up).

2 I _____ (not go) to school because I _____ (not feel) very well. My mother _____ (phone) the school in the afternoon and _____ (told) my teacher I was ill.

3 When they _____ (arrive), they _____ (give) me a present and _____ (take) me to the cinema – and it _____ (not be) my birthday!

4 She _____ (not come) to my party because she _____ (have) a headache.

5 They _____ (save) their money and _____ (go) on a big holiday.

2 Use the notes to write in the Past tense about Teresa's visit to London.

1 Teresa/wake up/7.00/have breakfast
2 she/go to London by train
3 she/visit the Tower of London
4 she/stop/for lunch near the river
5 she/leave/5.00/arrive home/6.30

3 Write about what you did or didn't do yesterday.

1 I _____ (wake up) at 5 o'clock.
2 I _____ (have) a big breakfast.
3 I _____ (feel) tired.
4 I _____ (phone) my friend.
5 I _____ (go) out in the evening.

4 Complete the sentences with comparative adjectives.

1 Fruit is _____ (healthy) than sweets.
2 I think mathematics is _____ (boring) than science.
3 Are people _____ (friendly) there?
4 Brazil are _____ (good) than our team.
5 The trains in London were _____ (expensive) than the trains in Madrid.

5 Write sentences about these things. Use comparative adjectives.

1 your language/English (easy)
2 London/New York (big)
3 art/music (interesting)
4 your country/Britain (small)
5 heavy metal/classical music (good)

Vocabulary

6 Identify the jobs.

lubmacena vreidr a_____ d_____

ootcrd d_____

reif ghfitre f_____ f_____

esrun n_____

ceilop fferioc p_____ o _____

7 Find the four seasons and five weather words.

S	N	O	S	N	O	W
U	W	I	P	M	R	I
N	I	A	R	U	C	N
N	N	R	I	T	O	H
Y	T	S	N	U	L	O
T	E	Y	G	A	D	P
S	R	E	M	M	U	S

Pronunciation

8 🔊 Listen and repeat.

Group 1 /ð/: that, their, then, there, they
Group 2 /θ/: thank, theatre, thing, think, three

9 Can you say this?

They think that there are three theatres.

Culture Corner 7

Strange but True

- There are four million cats in Britain, but over six million people say they have got a pet cat! Why? Some cats have more than one owner!

- Police officers in Britain are traditionally called bobbies. Why? The police force was started by Robert Peel in 1829 – and 'Bobby' is short for 'Robert'!

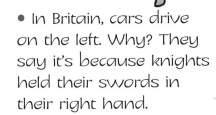

- In Britain, cars drive on the left. Why? They say it's because knights held their swords in their right hand.

1 Read the strange facts about Britain. Use the Mini-dictionary to help you.

2 Tell the class some strange things about your country. Can you explain them?

Learning Power!

Using a Dictionary

A dictionary tells you how to pronounce a word and what the word means. It also tells you what kind of word it is.

1 Match the numbers with these kinds of words:

noun / pronoun / verb / adjective / preposition

a) She   misses   Italian   food.
   1   2   3   4
b) He   drinks   hot   coffee   for   breakfast.
   1   2   3   4   5   6
c) She   goes   to   noisy   discos.
   1   2   3   4   5
d) He   plays   football   on   Sundays.
   1   2   3   4   5
e) They   wear   blue   uniforms   at   school.
   1   2   3   4   5   6

tug-of-war

15 Tests

In this module you ...

- **Read about** and **listen to** TV game shows and a dialogue.
- **Talk about** exams and your weekends.
- **Write** a quiz.
- **Learn about** *going to*, *have to* and *don't have to*.

Warm-up

1 **Check the meaning of the Key Words. Listen and repeat.**

KEY WORDS

fitness, intelligence, knowledge, memory, speed, strength

chess

2 What do the things in the photos test?

3 Read the questionnaire. Think about your answers.

QUESTIONNAIRE

1 What is your favourite sport? _____

2 What does it test? _____

3 What is your favourite TV game show?

_____

4 What does it test? _____

5 Do you play computer games?

Yes ☐   No ☐

6 What is your favourite game? _____

7 What does it test? _____

8 Do you do crosswords?   Yes ☐ No ☐

9 What do you think they test? _____

10 Where do you study for exams?

in the library ☐   in the playground ☐

in your bedroom ☐   in your sitting room ☐

on the bus ☐

Now work in pairs. Do the questionnaire with your partner.

Example

My favourite sport is swimming. It tests your fitness and strength. And you?

103

29 Exams

Before you start

1 Read the 'Top Tips'. Tick (✓) the things you do. Cross (✗) the things you don't do.

TOP TIPS FOR EXAM REVISION

1 Make a revision timetable. ☐

2 Look through your vocabulary notebook and mark important words. ☐

3 Look at the grammar sections of your coursebook. ☐

4 Study with a friend. Test his/her vocabulary and read his/her compositions. ☐

5 Leave some time to relax. ☐

6 Do some physical exercise (e.g. walking or swimming) – this helps you revise. ☐

7 Ask your teacher about things you don't understand. ☐

Reading and Listening

2. 🔊 Read the dialogue. Now listen and note the five differences.

Gabriela: Hi, Paola.

Paola: Hi, Gabi.

Gabriela: Our teacher is going to give us exams this week.

Paola: Yes, I know. When is she going to do the listening test?

Gabriela: She isn't going to do a listening test. We had one (1) <u>last week</u>, remember?

Paola: Oh, yes, that's (2) <u>good</u>. Er, are you going to see Adam tomorrow?

Gabriela: You mean after (3) <u>lunch</u>? No, I'm not going to see him tomorrow. I'm going to study for the exams.

Paola: Good idea. Well, we're going to have the class party on (4) <u>Friday</u> or (5) <u>Saturday</u>. You can see him at the party.

Gabriela: Yes, maybe. Kostas is going to ask Megan to go with him.

Paola: Really? Is Jamie going to come too?

Gabriela: I don't know. Why? Do you want him to come?

Paola: No. Well, maybe ...

going to FOR FUTURE PLANS
Presentation

3 Look at the examples with your teacher.

Affirmative

I'**m going to** study for the exams tomorrow.
Kostas **is going to** ask Megan to go with him on Friday.
We'**re going to** have the class party on Thursday.

Negative

I'**m not going to** see him tomorrow.

She **isn't going to** do a listening test this week.

Questions

When **is she going to** do the listening test?
Are you **going to** see Adam tomorrow?
Is Jamie **going to** come too?

[oo] Listen and repeat.

Practice

4 Write sentences.

Example
1 *I'm going to stay in tonight.*

1 I/stay in/tonight
2 you/come/to my party?
3 she/study/hard for the exam
4 he/watch/the match?
5 we/visit/the museum
6 they/not talk/in class

5 Write your diary with plans for this weekend. Include one false thing.

Example

FRIDAY

p.m. *do my homework*

SATURDAY

a.m. *help Mum with the shopping*
p.m. *stay at home*

SUNDAY

a.m. *tidy my room*
p.m. *study for the science test*

6 Work in pairs. Ask your partner what he/she is *going to* do this weekend. Then guess the false information.

Example
A: *What are you going to do on Friday night?*
B: *I'm going to do my homework.*

Prepositions

7 Preposition Review. Choose the correct prepositions.

Time

1 I'm going to finish my project *at/in/on* Saturday.
2 The film starts *at/in/on* 8 o'clock.
3 We're going to play tennis *at/in/on* the weekend.
4 She went to London *at/in/on* the summer.
5 My birthday is *at/in/on* the 21st March.
6 *At/In/On* Saturdays I work *at/in/on* the afternoon and I go out *at/in/on* night.
7 I go to school *after/before* breakfast.

Place

8 I've got a computer *at/in/on* my bedroom.
9 There are posters of pop stars *at/in/on* the wall.
10 My desk is *near/next* the window.

Movement

11 I arrived *at/to* school late.
12 I went *at/to* a coffee bar for lunch.

☞ Now do *Extra Time 29* on page 124.

30 Game Shows

Before you start

1 Do you like TV game shows? What are your favourites? Tell the class.

A–Z

2 Look at the Key Words. How do the people in the photos feel?

KEY WORDS

bored, disappointed, excited, nervous, relaxed

 Listen and repeat.

Reading and Listening

3 Read the texts. What game show tests your:

1 knowledge of prices and shopping?
2 general knowledge?
3 knowledge of songs and music?

1

2

3

A ## Who Wants To Be A Millionaire?

You **have to** answer fifteen questions to win £1 million – easy? No! The questions start easy and then get difficult.

With a difficult question, you can:
- ask the audience – they **have to** choose A, B, C or D, but you **don't have to** accept their answer
- phone a friend – he or she **has to** give you an answer in thirty seconds
- ask the presenter to take away two wrong answers

You get money for each correct answer. You **don't have to** answer all the questions – you can stop before the £1 million question.

B ## Name That Tune

*In this programme, you listen to the first notes of a song and you **have to** guess the song.*

4 Listen to the game shows. Match them to the texts.

C ## The Price Is Right

'Come on down, Sylvia Thomas!' shouts the presenter. Sylvia **has to** join three other people to play the first part of the game. She **has to** guess the price of an object, for example, a camera or a bag, but she **doesn't have to** guess the exact price. The winner plays the second part of the game to win a big prize.

4

5

have/has to, don't/doesn't have to
Presentation

5 Look at the examples with your teacher.

Affirmative
You **have to** answer fifteen questions correctly.
He or she **has to** give you an answer in thirty seconds.

Negative
You **don't have to** accept their answer.
She **doesn't have to** guess the exact price.

Questions
Do I **have to** give the singer's name?
Does it **have to** be the exact price?

⌷⌷ Listen and repeat.

Practice

6 Complete the sentences with *have to, has to, don't have to, doesn't have to, do* or *does.*

A: She (1) _____ answer this question – she can take the money.
B: I know, but to win a big prize, she (2) _____ give the correct answer.

C: (3) _____ I (4) _____ run in the race?
D: No, you (5) _____ run. You can watch.

E: What (6) _____ they (7) _____ do in this game?
F: They (8) _____ choose letters from a box and then make a word.

G: How long (9) _____ our project (10) _____ be?
H: Well, it (11) _____ be about five pages.

I: (12) _____ we (13) _____ do all the exercises?
J: No, you (14) _____ do exercises 5 and 6.

7 Write sentences about what you *have to* do at home. You can use these ideas:

tidy your room, clean the car, do your homework, take the dog for a walk, help with the shopping, wash the dishes, look after your little brother/sister, tidy the garden

Example
I have to tidy my room every weekend. I don't have to clean the car.

Speaking

8 Work in pairs. Talk about the things in Exercise 7.

Example
A: *I have to tidy my room every weekend.*
B: *I don't. But I have to clean our car on Saturdays!*

Now tell the class about your partner.

Example
Sue has to tidy her room every weekend. She doesn't have to clean the car.

☞ **Now do** *Extra Time 30* **on page 124.**

Communication Workshop

Writing: A Quiz

1 Work in pairs. Find the answers to these questions in the book.

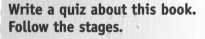

OPPORTUNITIES QUIZ

1 Who do Gabriela and Paola stay with?
2 What was the top name for a boy in Britain in 1998?
3 How many dogs does Gabriela have?
4 What are their names?
5 Who plays the piano – Gabriela or Paola?
6 What English football team does Kostas like?
7 What is the name of the river in Cambridge?
8 Where are Mr and Mrs Williams from?
9 When was Adam's accident?
10 What rare European animal lives in Poland?

Write a quiz about this book. Follow the stages.

Stage 1

Work in pairs. Look at the lessons in the book (including Culture Corners). Write ten quiz questions. Note the page numbers of the answers.

Stage 2

Check your questions for:
spelling ✓
grammar ✓

Speaking: Team Game

Test your friends about the book. Follow the stages.

Stage 1

Work in groups with another pair. One pair is Team A, one pair is Team B.

Stage 2

Take turns to ask and answer your questions. You have to answer in one minute!

Points
- you get five points for an answer without looking at the book
- you get one point if you have to look at the book
- you get no points if you can't answer

Talkback
Who got the most points in the class?

16 Goodbye

In this module you ...

- **Read** a poster and **listen to** dialogues.
- **Roleplay** a party, **make** suggestions, say *thanks* and *goodbye*.
- **Write** a party poster.
- **Learn about** making suggestions and revise verb forms.

Warm-up

 pages 26–27

1 🔊 **Check the meaning of the Key Words. Listen and repeat.**

KEY WORDS

crying, kissing goodbye, shaking hands, smiling, waving, hugging

What actions can you see in the photos?

Example
1 *They are waving goodbye.*

2 **What do *you* do when you say goodbye to these people? Tell the class.**

a) your parents b) your friends
c) your boyfriend/girlfriend   d) your teacher

Example
a) *I kiss and hug my parents.*

3 🔊 **Read and listen.**

Dialogue 1 (formal)
A: *Goodbye.*
B: *Goodbye. It was nice to meet you.*
A: *Yes, goodbye.*

Dialogue 2 (informal)
A: *Bye, Sarah.*
B: *Bye, Tom. Call me.*
A: *OK. See you!*

Work in pairs. Act out the dialogues.

31 Party Time

Before you start

A–Z

1 🔊 Check the meaning of the Key Words. Listen and repeat.

KEY WORDS

Food and drink:
cake, Coke, crisps, fruit juice, nuts, sandwiches

Music:
classical, heavy metal, salsa, techno

What food, drink and music do you like?

Reading and Listening

2 🔊 Read and listen. Complete the dialogue with the Key Words.

Kostas: OK, what type of music have we got?

Paola: Well, I've got some (1) _____ CDs, but they aren't good for a party! Why don't you bring your CDs, Gabriela?

Gabriela: Yes, sure. I've got some (2) _____ and techno.

Adam: And I've got my (3) _____ cassettes.

Paola: Oh, no Adam. Not AC/DC, please!

Gabriela: What about food and drink?

Kostas: Why don't we make some (4) _____ at home?

Adam: Yes, and we can buy (5) _____ , (6) _____ and Coke.

Kostas: I hate Coke.

Paola: Well, you can drink (7) _____ .

Gabriela: Let's buy a (8) _____ for the teacher, you know, to say 'thank you'.

Adam: That's a great idea, Gabi.

SUGGESTIONS
Presentation

3 Look at the examples with your teacher.

Why	**don't**	I/you/we/you/they	**bring** some CDs?
Why	**doesn't**	he/she	**make** some sandwiches?
Let's	**buy** a cake.		

🔊 Listen and repeat.

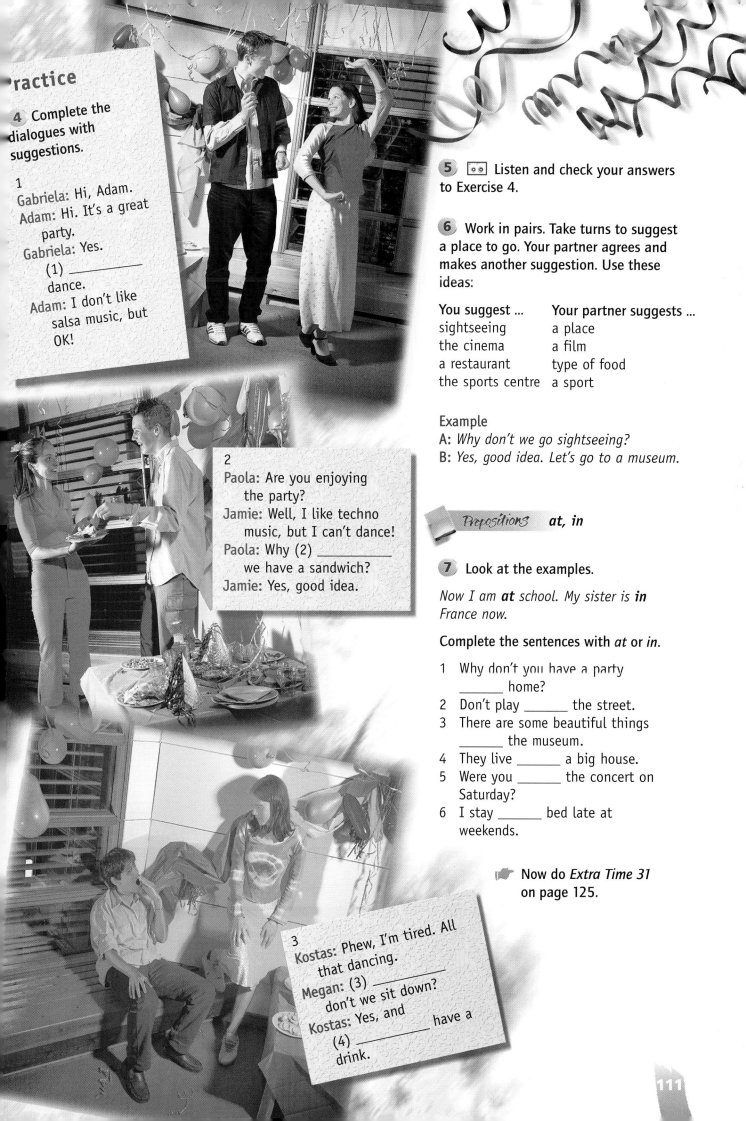

Practice

4 Complete the dialogues with suggestions.

1
Gabriela: Hi, Adam.
Adam: Hi. It's a great party.
Gabriela: Yes. (1) _____ dance.
Adam: I don't like salsa music, but OK!

2
Paola: Are you enjoying the party?
Jamie: Well, I like techno music, but I can't dance!
Paola: Why (2) _____ we have a sandwich?
Jamie: Yes, good idea.

3
Kostas: Phew, I'm tired. All that dancing.
Megan: (3) _____ don't we sit down?
Kostas: Yes, and (4) _____ have a drink.

5 🔊 Listen and check your answers to Exercise 4.

6 Work in pairs. Take turns to suggest a place to go. Your partner agrees and makes another suggestion. Use these ideas:

You suggest ...	Your partner suggests ...
sightseeing	a place
the cinema	a film
a restaurant	type of food
the sports centre	a sport

Example
A: *Why don't we go sightseeing?*
B: *Yes, good idea. Let's go to a museum.*

Prepositions **at, in**

7 Look at the examples.

Now I am **at** *school. My sister is* **in** *France now.*

Complete the sentences with *at* or *in*.

1 Why don't you have a party _____ home?
2 Don't play _____ the street.
3 There are some beautiful things _____ the museum.
4 They live _____ a big house.
5 Were you _____ the concert on Saturday?
6 I stay _____ bed late at weekends.

☞ Now do *Extra Time 31* on page 125.

111

32 Saying Goodbye

Reading and Listening

1 🔊 Read and listen. Complete the dialogues with these words:

> goodbye, not at all, thanks, address, have, see

1
Paola: (1) _____ for everything, Mrs Williams. It was a great holiday.
Gabriela: Yes, thank you.
Mrs Williams: (2) _____ .
Come again next year!
Paola: Bye!
Gabriela: Bye!

2
Megan: Can I have your e-mail (3) _____ ?
Kostas: Sure. It's easy. It's 'kdimitriou@prizma.gr'.
That's K – D – I – M – I – T – R – I – O – U
at P – R – I – Z – M – A dot G – R. What's your address?
Megan: It's 'mwilliams@red.uk'.
That's M – W – I – L – L – I – A – M – S at
R – E – D dot U – K.
Kostas: Thanks.

3
Jamie: Well, goodbye Paola. My dad's waiting for us in the car.
Paola: Bye, Jamie. It was a great holiday.
Come and (4) _____ me in Siena!
Jamie: Thanks. (5) _____ a good trip.

4
Adam: I don't like goodbyes but ... Oh no ... here's our taxi to the station.
Gabriela: OK, Adam. (6) _____ . Write to me!
Adam: Sure. Well ... bye Gabi!
Gabriela: Bye!

REVISION: VERB FORMS
Presentation

2 Match the sentences and the verb forms.

1 **Come** and see me in Siena!	a) present of *to be*
2 My dad**'s waiting** for us.	b) Imperative
3 It**'s** easy.	c) Present Simple
4 It **was** a great holiday.	d) Present Continuous
5 I **don't like** goodbyes.	e) Past Simple
6 The driver **stopped**.	f) *was/were*

Listen and repeat.

Practice

3 Complete the sentences with the correct form of the verbs in brackets.

1   _____ (not play) your CD, please. I _____ (study) for my exam.
2   The sports centre _____ (open) at 10 o'clock at the weekend.
3   Kostas _____ (be) from Greece.
4   How often _____ you _____ (go) to the cinema?
5   Let's go out – it _____ (not rain) now.
6   It _____ (be) a good match yesterday.
7   She _____ (get up) at 7 o'clock.
8   We _____ (be) tired yesterday.
9   He _____ (watch) TV last night.
10 He _____ (not work) at weekends.

4 Work in groups. Play the game. Go round the board three times.

- the first time, in the Present Simple
- the second time, in the Present Continuous
- the third time with an Imperative

Make sentences with the verbs. You get points for correct sentences.

Example
*I **get up** at 8 o'clock. My uncle in Australia **is getting up** now. **Get up!** It's late!*

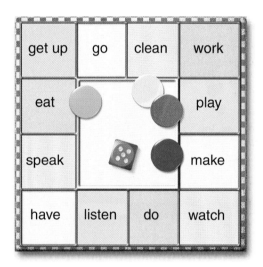

get up	go	clean	work
eat			play
speak			make
have	listen	do	watch

5 Work in pairs. Take turns to be the visitor and his/her English friend.

English friend	Visitor
ask for e-mail address	give address and spell it – ask for friend's
give address and spell it – tell him/her to write	thank him/her for the holiday
reply ask him/her to come again	say the train/ bus/taxi is here
say goodbye	say goodbye

Now do *Extra Time 32* on page 125.

Communication Workshop

PARTY

Do you want to dance (1)

Do you want to meet new friends (2)

Do you want to listen to techno and rap music (3)

Come to our party (4)

It's on Friday at 8 o'clock in the school coffee bar.

Good food – pizza and cakes (5)

Bring a friend (6)

No parents (7)

Don't be late (8)

Writing: A Party Poster

1 Complete the poster with question marks or exclamation marks.

Design a poster for a party at your school. Follow the stages.

Stage 1
Write notes for your party.

music, food, time, day, place

Stage 2
Design your poster. Write questions and exclamations.

Stage 3
Check your poster for:
spelling ✓ punctuation ✓

Talkback
In groups, read your friends' posters. Which party do you want to go to?

Speaking: A Roleplay

Act out a party situation. Follow the stages.

Stage 1
Work in groups. Write this information on a piece of paper.

name, age, job, country

Example
Michelle/36/actress/Australia

Stage 2
Mix up the pieces of paper. Take turns to choose a 'role'. This is your new identity.

Stage 3
Imagine you are at a party. Talk to the others and ask questions.

Example
Hi. My name's Michelle. I'm an actress. What's your name?

Talkback
Tell the class about a person at the party.

Example
Gary is a football player from Scotland. He's twenty-five.

Review

Grammar

1 Complete the sentences with the correct form of *have to.*

1 We _____ go to school on Sundays.
2 You _____ wait – you can go now.
3 He _____ help with the cleaning to get pocket money.
4 _____ you _____ wear school uniform?
5 He _____ work because he's rich.
6 She _____ work very hard because she's got a big family.

2 Complete the letter with the verbs in the correct form.

Dear Greg,

How (1) _____ (be) you? Thanks for the photo of you and your dog. I (2) _____ (not like) dogs, but my mother (3) _____ (think) they (4) _____ (be) great. Every day she (5) _____ (go) for a walk with her friend's dog.

What (6) _____ (be) your exams like last month? We (7) _____ (have got) exams in school this week. We (8) _____ (have) a science exam yesterday it (9) _____ (be) horrible!

My brother (10) _____ (have got) a new CD player. He and his friend (11) _____ (play) techno pop at the moment in his bedroom. I (12) _____ (hate) techno music - and he (13) _____ (not like) my heavy metal cassettes.

Anyway, why (14) _____ you _____ (come) to visit me this summer? There (15) _____ (be) some good places to go - the beach and the sports centre - and a new disco (16) _____ (open) in town next week. Let's (17) _____ (talk) to our parents about it.

Write soon!

Bye!

Mark.

P.S. (18) _____ (not forget) to write to Sandra. I (19) _____ (see) her last week and she (20) _____ (miss) you!

Vocabulary

3 Complete the sentences with these words.

bored, excited, happy, nervous, relaxed, angry, late

1 I was really _____ before the exam but when it started I was more _____ .
2 She was _____ and _____ when she passed the exam.
3 I'm sorry I'm _____ . Are you _____ ?
4 They were _____ at the party – the music was bad.

4 Find twelve names of food and drink.

C	R	I	S	P	S	O
H	A	C	E	W	A	R
E	B	A	N	A	N	A
E	C	K	U	T	D	N
S	A	E	T	E	W	G
E	G	G	S	R	I	E
E	E	F	F	O	C	O
S	A	L	A	D	H	C

Pronunciation

5 Listen Listen and repeat the words.

Group 1 /d/: dancing, disco, drink, food, good, idea
Group 2 /t/: cassette, let's, nuts, party, take, techno, that, water

6 Listen Now listen and repeat these sentences.

1 That's a good idea.
2 Let's take your cassettes to the party.
3 I like dancing to techno music.

Now read the story **Money Talks** on pages 126–127.

Culture Corner 8

Important Dates in Multicultural Britain

Chinese New Year.
21 January – 19 February.
Chinese people in Britain decorate their houses with flowers. They carry a paper dragon in the streets of big cities like Manchester for the Lantern Festival.

Valentine's Day.
14 February.
Young people send cards to someone they love – and they don't put their name!

Easter. March or April.
An important Christian festival. Children also eat chocolate eggs at Easter.

Diwali. 26 October.
The New Year Festival of Lights for the Hindu community in Britain.

Christmas Day.
25 December.
People celebrate the birth of Jesus and give presents.

New Year. 31 December – 1 January.
People go to parties and celebrate the New Year. In Scotland they call it 'Hogmanay'.

Ramadan.
Ramadan is important for the big Muslim community in Britain. They don't eat during the day. At the end of Ramadan there are three days of celebration.

1 Read about festivals in Britain. Use the Mini-dictionary to help you.

2 Answer these questions.

1 Do you have the same festivals in your country?
2 Write the dates of some important festivals in your country.

Learning Power!

Self-evaluation and revision

1 Mark your progress in these areas. Be honest!

speaking ☐   reading ☐   writing ☐   listening ☐
grammar ☐   vocabulary ☐   pronunciation ☐

Key
3 very good
2 OK
1 not very good

Which area do you want to practise more?

2 Read the advice about exams.

- Don't try to do all your revision the night before!
- Look at your writing and tests and identify your problem areas.
- Look at the grammar boxes and your example sentences.
- Look at your vocabulary book and the Mini-dictionary.

116

Extra Time!

1 Flag Quiz

Write down the names of the countries.

Example
1 *Australia*

2 Star Quiz

Match the stars and their nationalities.

Example
Pavarotti – Italy

American, Australian, Italian, French, British, Russian, Spanish, Brazilian

3 Family Puzzle

Read the puzzle. Complete the family tree.

Tom =

PUZZLE

1 My name is Susan. My father is Tom.
2 My name is Judy. My daughters are Lucy and Susan.
3 My name is Sam. My mother is Judy.
4 My name is Lucy. My brothers are Sam and Nick.
5 My name is Tom. My parents are John and Mary.
6 My name is Mary. My children are Sally and Tom.
7 My name is John. My grandsons are Sam and Nick.

4 Job Search

Look at the pictures and find seven jobs.

Example
1 *a scientist*

5 Home Puzzle

Find these words.

bath, bed, computer, cooker, fridge, lamp, shower, sofa, television, toilet, window

T	O	I	L	E	T	A	B
E	T	E	B	A	R	S	C
L	E	G	E	M	E	H	O
E	I	D	P	U	T	O	M
V	W	I	N	D	O	W	P
I	E	R	O	H	S	E	U
S	O	F	A	O	H	R	T
I	B	A	T	H	O	B	E
O	E	C	O	O	K	E	R
N	D	E	P	M	A	L	K

6 A Description

Use the pictures to write a description of a bedroom.

My room has got walls.

I've got posters of

and my favourite on the walls.

The room has got a big .

It's got a

for my and my .

My new  is great.

I've got a on my

7 Odd One Out

Circle the 'odd one out'.

Example

1 Athens is not a country.

1 Argentina, Athens, Italy, Poland
2 actor, doctor, engineer, school
3 class, geography, history, science
4 mother, sister, son, wife

Write an 'odd one out' for your friend.

8 Hidden Words

Find things in the classroom.

Example 1 desk

1	keds	5	estasect
2	dobar	6	eshfl
3	voide	7	crityondia
4	kobo	8	podcubar

9 Spot the Places!

Find places in the street. Then write sentences.

Example

Go to the Odeon Cinema. It's got interesting films. Don't go to the Clifton Cinema. Their films are terrible!

10 Find the Objects

Find and list twelve hidden objects in the picture.

Example *two sandwiches*

11 Find the Activities

Look at the drawing. Find eight sports activities.

Example
1 *do the high jump*

12 A Busy Family!

Read about the family. At what times can the four people in the family meet? Complete the sentence.

They can meet from _____ to _____ and from _____ to _____ .

Jacky: *at school – 9.00 a.m.–3.30 p.m./ at home – 4.00–6.00 p.m./ at swimming class – 6.00–7.00 p.m./at home – 7.15 p.m. –*

Tim: *at university – 10 a.m.–5.00 p.m./ at home – 5.15–6.30 p.m./at the gym – 6.30–8.00 p.m./ at home – 8.15–9.30 p.m./ out with friends 9.30 p.m.–1.00 a.m./at home – 1.00 a.m. –*

Mum: *at work – 7.00 a.m.–5.00 p.m./at home – 5.15 p.m.*

Dad: *at work – 8.30 a.m.–5.30 p.m./at home – 5.45 p.m. –*

13 Puzzle

Write the other days of the week in the squares.

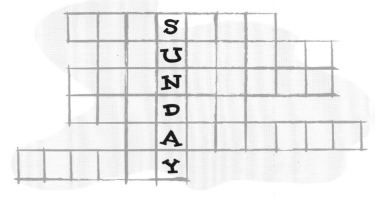

14 A Typical Day

Put the activities in order for a typical day for you.

- [ ] I have a shower.
- [ ] I have lunch.
- [ ] I get up.
- [ ] I do my homework.
- [ ] I have breakfast.
- [ ] I go home.
- [ ] I clean my teeth.
- [ ] I go to school.

Add two more activities you do on a typical day.
I _____ and I _____ .

15 Questionnaire

Complete the questionnaire.

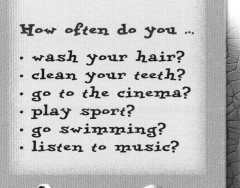

How often do you ...

- wash your hair?
- clean your teeth?
- go to the cinema?
- play sport?
- go swimming?
- listen to music?

Now interview another student.

16 Word Snake

Find activities in the word snake.

listentomusicollecttthingsurfthqeinternetakephotoswim

Example
listen to music

Write your own word snake with English words.

17 Family Favourites

Look at the picture of the family. Write about their activities.

Example
Mum is eating an apple.
She is ...

18 People Puzzle

Look at the pictures and read the descriptions. Name the people.

1   2   3

Tim is wearing a hat. He isn't wearing a jumper.
He is wearing a T-shirt. He isn't wearing jeans.

Tom is wearing a hat. He isn't wearing a jumper.
He is wearing a T-shirt. He isn't wearing shorts.

Sam is wearing a hat. He isn't wearing shorts.
He is wearing jeans. He isn't wearing a T-shirt.

19 Wildlife

Put the animals in the correct column.

> hippo, kangaroo, koala, lion,
> llama, panda, tiger, zebra

Africa	Asia	Australia	South America

Can you add more animals to the list?

20 Animal Quiz

Guess the animals.

1 This animal isn't very big. It isn't very rare. It hasn't got long legs. It's got very big eyes. It lives in trees in Australia. It is a

_____ .

2 This animal is black and white. It isn't very rare. It has got a big body and a small head. It is a bird but it can't fly. It can't run fast but it can swim fast. It lives in Antarctica and South America. It is a _____ .

3 This animal is very big. It has got a big head and long legs. It is orange and black.
It is a big cat. It can run very fast. It lives in Asia. It is now very rare. It is a _____ .

4 This animal is big. It is a bird. It has got small eyes but they are very good. It has got very big wings. It is very rare. It lives in Europe and Asia. It is a

_____ .

5 This animal is not very rare. It is huge and it hasn't got wings. It has got big ears. It lives in Africa. It can run very fast. People ride this animal. It is an

_____ .

Write an animal quiz using the pictures.

21 Book Quiz

What can you remember? Are these sentences about the characters in the book true (T) or false (F)?

1 Gabriela and Paola were at the railway station (in Module 5).
2 Kostas and Adam were at a newsagent's (in Module 5).
3 Gabriela and Paola were at the market (in Module 5).
4 Adam and Gabriela were at the swimming pool (in Module 6).
5 Kostas and Megan were at the sports centre (in Module 6).
6 Gabriela and Adam were at the cinema (in Module 8).
7 The four students were at the British Museum (in Module 9).
8 The four students were at Buckingham Palace (in Module 9).
9 The four students were in Trafalgar Square (in Module 9).
10 The four students were at a wildlife park (in Module 10).

22 First Memories

Read the first memories. Who are the characters from the book?

1 I remember my first memory very well. I think I was three. I was at home. I was on the balcony. I was with my dad. My mother was at her desk, translating a book. The weather was great! It was hot and sunny.

2 I was about three or four. I was in the garden with my brother and my dad. It was very cold and rainy. Ah yes! Toby was in the garden. He was a puppy.

3 In my first memory I was four. I was at home with my dad. He was on the sofa. I was on the floor with my cat Leo. He was a kitten.

23 Word Puzzle

Use the letters to make place words from the lesson.

1 m a s t u m e n e   e r a c d a
2 w o n l i b g   l a y e l
3 m a n i c e
4 f e c o f e   r a b
5 c e r n c o t
6 a r b r i l y

Write a word puzzle for another student.

24 Guess the Programme

Identify the kind of TV programme.

1 The habitat of the Imperial Eagle is disappearing and this bird is now very rare. Alistair Cummins looks at the problem.
2 Alice is not very happy. Where is her letter from Sebastian? It is not in her desk. Andy comes home but his parents are very angry. Judy meets Tim at the coffee bar.
3 Wimbledon 2001 – Venus Williams vs. Monica Seles.
4 Today's news and weather from the Midlands area.
5 A brilliant western with John Wayne and James Stewart.
6 The Hopkiss family have fun again! Uncle Graham can't find his false teeth. Very funny!

25 Odd One Out

Find the 'odd one out'.

1 ambulance, fire engine, bicycle, police car
2 hospital, cinema, doctor, police station
3 bicycle, cyclist, driver, helmet
4 helmet, hospital, medicine, nurse
5 arrived, left, stopped, turned
6 asked, gave, saw, wore

26 At the Doctor's

Write sentences about the people at the doctor's.

Example
The young woman is very happy.

27 Adjectives

Change the adjectives to their opposites.

I had a really <u>bad</u> holiday. The weather was <u>cold</u>. Our hotel room was <u>small</u> and the people were <u>unfriendly</u>. And, of course, the language is really <u>hard</u> to understand.

28 British and American English

Match the British and American English words.

British English	American English
1 autumn	a) cookie
2 biscuit	b) vacation
3 film	c) gas
4 holiday	d) fall
5 lift	e) truck
6 lorry	f) candy
7 petrol	g) movie
8 shop	h) cab
9 sweets	i) store
10 taxi	j) elevator

29 Vocabulary Table

Can you complete the table? Try it with different letters.

	C	A	R
Animal		ant	
Adjective	cold		
Country	China		
Food and Drink			ravioli
Verb			run

30 Word Puzzle

Make words from the letters. There is one nine-letter word.

D	W	S
N	E	A
E	Y	D

Score: two-letter words = 2 points, three-letter words = 3 points, etc.

31 Party Questionnaire

Answer the questionnaire.

1 **Where do you go to parties?**
a) at home b) at a friend's house c) at school d) at discos

2 **What time do you have parties?**
a) in the afternoon b) after 6 o'clock c) after 10.00p.m.

3 **Do you like parties?**
a) yes b) no c) some parties

4 **What do you do at parties?**
a) dance all the time b) dance and talk c) sit and talk

5 **Who do you talk to?**
a) all the people b) my friends c) one or two people

6 **What do you like drinking?**
a) Coke b) fruit juice c) water

7 **What music do you like?**
a) techno b) salsa c) heavy metal d) rock

8 **What do you wear at parties?**
a) jeans and a T-shirt b) formal clothes

32 Flights Home

It was impossible for Kostas, Adam and Gabriela to get direct flights from London. Find their flights home.

Example
Kostas: (1) British Airways – London – Athens (2) Olympic Airways …

Aerolineas Argentinas:	Leave Madrid 22.35/ Arrive Buenos Aires 06.15 (next day)
British Airways:	Leave London Heathrow 10.30/Arrive Athens 14.30
LOT Polish Airways:	Leave Zurich 20.00/Arrive Warsaw 22.15
Olympic Airways:	Leave Athens 18.00/Arrive Rhodes 19.10
British Airways:	Leave London Gatwick 19.10/Arrive Madrid 21.00
Swiss Air:	Leave London Heathrow 12.00/Arrive Zurich 14.30

What person:

a) gets home first? b) gets home last? c) has a long wait?

Story Spot

Money Talks

Before you start

❶ Look at the drawings in the story. Which of these things do you think it is about?

a) money problems
b) love
c) a son's problems with his father
d) love and money

Reading and Listening

❷ 🔈 Read and listen to the story. Check your answers to Exercise 1.

❸ Read the story again. Are these sentences True or False?

1 Old Mr Rockwall thinks money is very important.
2 Richard doesn't agree with him.
3 Richard is worried about his job.
4 Richard isn't happy because Ellen doesn't love him.
5 Ellen is going to go to Europe for a year.
6 Richard hasn't got time to talk to her before she goes.
7 Richard thinks money can solve his problem.
8 Richard arrives at Ellen's house very late.
9 They are late for the theatre because of the rain.
10 Ellen is angry because she can't go to the theatre.
11 Ellen and Richard talk and fall in love.
12 Mr Rockwall organised the traffic problems.
13 He gave $10 to the policemen to stop the traffic.
14 He is not very happy with Mr Kelly's work.
15 Mr Rockwall used his money to solve the problems.

❹ Does money 'talk'- is it very important in life? What do you think? Do you agree with Richard or his father?

Number 24 Park Street is a big, expensive house. Old Mr Anthony Rockwall lives there and he is very rich.

One day, he talks to his son, Richard. He is a quiet man of twenty-one. 'Richard, the people on this street come from good families and have a lot of money. We aren't a famous old family but we have a lot of money. Money can open a lot of doors for you,' Mr Rockwall says with a smile.

'It can open *some* doors, father, but not *every* door,' Richard says. 'Money can't buy a place at the table of the right people.'

'You're wrong, young man,' his father says and he looks into his son's eyes. Richard is quiet.

'Son, what's the problem? Are you sick? What's wrong? You can talk to me.' Mr Rockwall says.

'Father, I'm not sick. I have a good home, an interesting job, and a clever old father. But . . .'

'What's her name?' Mr Rockwall asks.

'Oh, Father. She's beautiful and very special. Her name is Ellen Lantry. She's the only woman for me.' Richard says.

'Talk to her. Dance with her. Walk in the rain with her. She's going to love you too,' his father

by O. Henry

says. 'You're a good young man. You're special too.'

'But she's always with people,' Richard says. 'I never have any time with her. She never has time for me.'

'Richard! Take some money and buy some time with her. Talk to her about your love,' the old man says.

'I can't,' Richard says. 'She's going to Europe by boat tomorrow. She's going to stay there for two years. This evening I'm going to take her to the theatre but it's a short drive. I'm not going to have much time with her and you can't buy *her* time.'

'OK, Richard, now I understand. Your love for her is very strong but she doesn't know about it. That's your problem,' Mr Rockwall says.

'She can't know because there isn't time,' Richard says. He's very unhappy. 'Your money can't talk to her.'

At eight o'clock in the evening, Richard goes to the beautiful young woman's house. 'Good evening, Richard,' Miss Lantry says. 'Mother and Father are waiting for us at the theatre. I don't want to be late.'

'To Wallack's Theatre, please,' Richard says to the driver. But at Thirty-fourth Street the car stops.

'What's wrong?' Richard asks.

'I'm sorry, Mr Rockwall,' the driver says. 'We can't move. The traffic is terrible.'

'Oh, Richard. Are we going to be late?' Miss Lantry asks.

'I'm very sorry, Ellen. No theatre for us this evening,' Richard says.

'That's OK. I don't like the theatre very much. I'm happy here in the car with you,' Miss Lantry says.

'Are you?' Richard asks with a smile.

Later in the evening Richard talks to his father. 'Father,' Richard says, 'Miss Lantry and I are in love!'

'Very good, Richard. I'm happy for you,' his father says.

'We talked and talked. She loves me! You see! Money can't buy love,' Richard says. Then the happy young man goes to bed.

But let's finish the story. At seven o'clock in the morning, the driver comes to the door of Mr Rockwall's house.

'Good morning, Mr Kelly,' Mr Rockwall says. 'You did a good job yesterday evening. Here's your $5,000.'

'It was difficult, Mr Rockwall. The drivers of the cars wanted $10 and the policemen wanted $50. But the cars stopped for us. Did it all go well?' Mr Kelly asks.

'Well? Yes! It was beautiful. Let's drink to love and to money!'

COMMUNICATION WORKSHOP
Speaking (Stage 1)

Student A - Paola's and Gabriela's area/house

Where - 20 minutes from city centre

Places:
disco x
cinema x
bookshop (1)
supermarket (1)
post office x
park (1)
gym (1)
restaurants - one Chinese restaurant
hotel x
church (1)
cafés (2)
museum x
banks (2)

COMMUNICATION WORKSHOP
Speaking (Stage 1)

Student B - Adam's and Kostas's area/house

Where - centre of Cambridge

Places:
parks (2)
restaurants (4)
cinemas (2)
discos (2)
museums (2)
banks (3)
bookshops (2)
post office x
supermarket (1)
cafés (4)
churches (3)

Pág 38 A Exercício

the town has got a three cafés.
but it hasn't got bookshop.

The town has got a post office
but it hasn't got books

The town has got a café.
but it hasn't got Hotel.